JN086657

kwaidan

by Koizumi Yakumo

Level 3
(1600-word)

Adapted by David Olivier

IBC パブリッシング

はじめに

　ラダーシリーズは、「はしご（ladder）」を使って一歩一歩上を目指すように、学習者の実力に合わせ、無理なくステップアップできるよう開発された英文リーダーのシリーズです。

　リーディング力をつけるためには、繰り返したくさん読むこと、いわゆる「多読」がもっとも効果的な学習法であると言われています。多読では、「1. 速く　2. 訳さず英語のまま　3. なるべく辞書を使わず」に読むことが大切です。スピードを計るなど、速く読むよう心がけましょう（たとえば TOEIC® テストの音声スピードはおよそ1分間に150語です）。そして1語ずつ訳すのではなく、英語を英語のまま理解するくせをつけるようにします。こうして読み続けるうちに語感がついてきて、だんだんと英語が理解できるようになるのです。まずは、ラダーシリーズの中からあなたのレベルに合った本を選び、少しずつ英文に慣れ親しんでください。たくさんの本を手にとるうちに、英文書がすらすら読めるようになってくるはずです。

《本シリーズの特徴》

- 中学校レベルから中級者レベルまで5段階に分かれています。自分に合ったレベルからスタートしてください。
- クラシックから現代文学、ノンフィクション、ビジネスと幅広いジャンルを扱っています。あなたの興味に合わせてタイトルを選べます。
- 巻末のワードリストで、いつでもどこでも単語の意味を確認できます。レベル1、2では、文中の全ての単語が、レベル3以上は中学校レベル外の単語が掲載されています。
- カバーにヘッドホーンマークのついているタイトルは、オーディオ・サポートがあります。ウェブから購入／ダウンロードし、リスニング教材としても併用できます。

《使用語彙について》

レベル1：中学校で学習する単語約1000語

レベル2：レベル1の単語＋使用頻度の高い単語約300語

レベル3：レベル1の単語＋使用頻度の高い単語約600語

レベル4：レベル1の単語＋使用頻度の高い単語約1000語

レベル5：語彙制限なし

CONTENTS

The Story of
Mimi-Nashi-Hoichi

The Story of Mimi-Nashi-Hoichi
耳なし芳一の話

The Story of Mimi-Nashi-Hoichi で使われている用語です。わからない語は巻末のワードリストで確認しましょう。

- ☐ blind
- ☐ force
- ☐ graveyard
- ☐ haunt
- ☐ interrupt
- ☐ lord
- ☐ palace
- ☐ servant
- ☐ spirit

●主な登場人物と作品の舞台

Hoichi 芳一　盲目の琵琶法師。弾き語りが非常に巧みである。

Priest 和尚　芳一を引き取り、面倒をみている阿弥陀寺の和尚。

samurai 侍　芳一を訪れ、「殿」の元で弾き語りをするよう求める。

Dan-no-ura 壇ノ浦　現在の山口県下関市の沖合。源氏と平家の最後の戦いの場となった。

●この作品の背景

源氏と平家の戦いの舞台となった壇ノ浦。この戦いにおいて平家は滅亡することになる。その平家の恨み、悲しみがこの物語を産んだと思われる。
なお、この舞台となった阿弥陀寺は、現在は「赤間神宮」となって残っている。

A great battle at Dan-no-ura, in the waters of Shimonoseki, was fought more than seven hundred years ago.

It was the last battle between the Heike, or Taira clan, and the Genji, or Minamoto clan. The Heike soldiers, women, and children were all killed. The young emperor, called Antoku Tenno, was killed too.

The shores of Shimonoseki are still haunted today. People say there are strange crabs there called Heike crabs, which are the spirits of the Heike soldiers. These crabs have human faces on their backs.

There are other strange things that happen on that coast. On dark nights, strange fires glow above the beach and the waves. The fishermen call them *Oni-bi*. And the wind makes a noise like the sound of a great battle.

In the past, the Heike were more active than they are now. They would often try to sink ships at night and pull swimmers under the sea.

Then, a temple called Amida-ji was built at Akamagaseki to make the spirits less angry. A graveyard was also built near there, with the names of the emperor and his subjects.

People would pray for the spirits too. Later the Heike caused less trouble, but they still were not at peace.

Hoichi was a blind man who lived at Akamagaseki many centuries ago. He was famous for his skill at telling stories and playing the *biwa*. He was best at singing the sad song of the battle of Dan-no-ura.

Hoichi was very poor until he became good friends with a priest from Amida-ji. This man liked Hoichi's stories and invited him to live in the temple. Hoichi was given a room and food in exchange for singing his stories.

One very hot summer night, the priest was

away and Hoichi was alone. Hoichi went outside to a cool porch overlooking the garden. He practiced his *biwa* while waiting for the priest to return. It was after midnight, but the priest was not back.

At last Hoichi heard someone coming through the back gate. This person crossed the garden and stopped in front of Hoichi—but it was not the priest. Then a deep, hard, voice, that sounded like a samurai, called out:

"Hoichi!"

Hoichi was too surprised to answer.

"Hoichi!"

"Yes!" answered the blind man, very afraid of this voice. "I am blind. I don't know you!"

"There is nothing to fear," said the stranger. "I have been sent to you with a message. My lord is a very important person now staying in Akamagaseki. He wanted to see the battle ground of Dan-no-ura and he went there today. He heard of your story-telling skill and wants to hear your song. So please come with me now to the house where my lord and his important friends are waiting."

Hoichi had to obey the orders of the samurai. He took the *biwa* and walked away with the stranger. The samurai was dressed in iron and was probably a palace guard. Hoichi began to think he was lucky. He imagined that the lord was probably a *daimyo*.

They came to a large gate. The only such gate that Hoichi knew of was the entrance to the Amida-ji.

"Kaimon! (Open the gate!)" the samurai called, and they passed through. They then crossed a garden and came to another doorway. "I have brought Hoichi," called the samurai.

The doors were opened and inside Hoichi heard women talking. Hoichi thought they were palace servants, but he didn't know where he was.

Then a woman took his hand and guided him on a long walk. They went along wooden floors and around many corners to a large room. By the sounds and voices around him Hoichi sensed that many great people were gathered there.

Hoichi was told to make himself comfortable. Someone gave him a soft seat to sit on. He then heard the voice of a woman who said:

"Now please play your *biwa* and tell us the story of the Heike."

The entire story was too long to tell in one evening, so Hoichi asked, "Which part of the story do you want to hear the most?"

The woman answered, "The sad, sad, story of the battle at Dan-no-ura."

Hoichi sang the tale of the bitter fight at sea. His *biwa* made the sounds of ships and wind and shouting and swords and death.

And he could hear those around him say, "He is a wonderful artist!" "I have never heard better!" "He is the greatest singer in the land!" This made Hoichi feel even better, and he played and sang like he had never done before.

At last he came to the saddest part of the story, when the women and children and the young emperor were killed. All the listeners held their breaths. Then they began to cry and weep. Hoichi was frightened. Slowly, the cries stopped and the woman again spoke to Hoichi.

"We were told that you play the *biwa* with great skill. However, you are better than we expected. Our lord is very pleased and he would like to reward you generously. But he wants you to perform for him every night for the next six nights. After that, he will return to his home. Tomorrow night you are to come here at the same time. The same man will bring you here. There is one more thing I must ask you. Do not tell anyone of your visit here. Our lord is traveling secretly and no one must know. You may now go back to your temple."

A servant then took Hoichi back through the palace. Outside, the samurai guided him back to the temple and said goodbye.

It was almost dawn when Hoichi returned to the temple. However, the priest had also returned very late. The priest thought Hoichi was sleeping. During the day Hoichi rested. He said nothing about his strange adventure.

The next night the samurai again came to get him. Hoichi played the *biwa* for the same important group. He was a great success.

Hoichi then returned to the temple. But this time someone had noticed that he had been missing at the temple. In the morning, the priest came to talk to him.

"We were very worried about you, Hoichi. To go out at night, blind and alone, is dangerous. Why did you go without telling us, and where did you go?"

Hoichi could not tell the truth. "I'm sorry, kind friend. I had some private business and it could not wait until morning."

The priest was surprised, and he guessed that something was wrong. He was afraid that the young blind man was affected by evil spirits. He asked no more questions, but he secretly asked some servants in the temple to watch where Hoichi went and follow him.

The next night, Hoichi was seen leaving the temple and the servants followed him. But it was rainy and very dark and they lost sight of him.

They were surprised at how quickly the blind man walked. They then walked through the town looking everywhere, but they couldn't find him. Then, as they were returning to the temple, they heard the loud sound of a *biwa*. They followed the sound into the Amida-ji graveyard, and there they found Hoichi.

He was sitting alone in the rain in front of the grave of Antoku Tenno. He was singing of the battle of Dan-no-ura. All around him the fires of the dead were burning above the graves. The men had never before seen so many *Oni-bi*.

"Hoichi-san! Hoichi-san!" the servants cried, "you are possessed by dead spirits!"

But the blind man continued to play his *biwa* and sing of the battle. The men then held him and shouted in his ear, "Hoichi-san! Come home with us at once!"

Hoichi said to them, "You must not interrupt me in front of such great people in this palace!"

The men then pulled him to his feet and forced Hoichi to return with them to the temple. They brought him dry clothes and gave him food and water. Then the priest demanded to hear the truth of what had happened.

Hoichi did not want to speak, but he knew the priest was very upset. At last, he told the priest everything.

The priest said, "Hoichi my poor friend, you are now in great danger. I wish you had told me earlier. Your skill in music has brought you trouble. Now you know that you have not been visiting a palace at night. Instead, you have been among the graves of the Heike. We found you sitting in the rain in front of Antoku Tenno's grave. When you obeyed the spirits, you put yourself in their power. If you obey them again they will destroy you. Now, I must leave again tonight to do something. But before I go, it will be necessary to protect you. I will write holy words on your body. That will protect you."

Before sunset the priest and his helper took off Hoichi's clothes. They then wrote the words of the Hannya-Shin-Kyo over every part of his body with their brushes. Soon Hoichi was completely covered with these words.

When this was done the priest told Hoichi, "Tonight, when I leave, you must sit on the garden porch and wait. You will be called. But whatever happens, don't answer, and don't move. If you move or make a noise you will be destroyed. Don't be afraid, and don't call for help. Nobody can help you. If you do exactly as I tell you the danger will go away and you will have nothing to fear."

After dark the priest and his helper went away.

Hoichi sat down on the garden porch. He put his *biwa* down next to him and waited. He was very still. He waited for hours.

Then, from the road, he heard the sound of someone coming. Someone passed the gate, crossed the garden to the porch, and stopped in front of Hoichi.

"Hoichi!" the deep voice called. But the blind man sat without moving or breathing.

"Hoichi!" came the voice a second time. Then, angrily, a third time, "Hoichi!!" But Hoichi did not move.

Then the voice said, "No answer! That is not good! I must find him."

Then Hoichi heard the sound of heavy feet walking onto the garden porch. The feet stopped beside him. There was dead silence for a long time.

At last he heard the voice next to him say, "Here is the *biwa*; but of the *biwa* player I see only two ears! So that explains why he did not answer—he has two ears but no mouth. Now I must take these ears to my lord. They will prove that I have obeyed his orders."

At that moment Hoichi felt fingers of iron hold his ears and tear them off! The pain was terrible, but Hoichi did not make a sound.

The heavy footsteps then walked away past the garden to the road and disappeared. Hoichi felt warm blood coming down both sides of his head but still he did not move....

Before sunrise the priest came back. He hurried to the garden porch and cried out in surprise when he saw Hoichi. Hoichi was sitting in a small pool of his own blood.

"My poor Hoichi!" cried the frightened priest. "You've been hurt.... What happened?"

At the sound of his friend's voice the blind man felt safe. He began to cry and he told the priest about his adventure that night.

"My poor, poor Hoichi!" the priest exclaimed. "This is all my fault. I am to blame. I trusted my helper to write the holy words all over your body, but he forgot to write them on your ears! I should have checked myself. Well, it's too late now. We can only try to make you feel better. The danger is over now, Hoichi. Those visitors will never bother you again."

With the help of a good doctor, Hoichi soon recovered from his wounds.

The story of his strange adventure spread everywhere, and he was soon famous. Many important people went to Akamagaseki to hear him sing and play the *biwa*.

He received large gifts of money and became a wealthy man. But ever since that night on the garden porch he was known as Mimi-nashi-Hoichi: "Hoichi the Earless."

Yuki-Onna

Yuki-Onna
雪女

Yuki-Onna で使われている用語です。わからない語は巻末のワードリストで確認しましょう。

- [ ] awful
- [ ] delay
- [ ] flood
- [ ] honorable
- [ ] praise
- [ ] remind
- [ ] senseless
- [ ] snowstorm
- [ ] woodcutter

●雪女伝説

雪女は「雪女子」「雪女郎」などとも呼ばれ、日本の雪国各地で伝承される雪の精霊。色白の美しい女性として語られることが多い。本作品は、八雲が西多摩郡調布（現在の東京都青梅市）の農民から村の伝説として聞いた話である。100年以上前の東京西部地方は豪雪地帯であり、八王子や青梅などには「雪女郎」伝説が残っている。

●主な登場人物と作品の舞台

Minokichi 巳之吉　若いきこり。年配のきこり、茂作と森から帰ってくる途中、吹雪に遭う。

O-Yuki お雪　色白の美しい女性。江戸に向かう途中、巳之吉の道連れとなる。

Musashi Province 武蔵国　旧国名のひとつ。現在の埼玉県、東京都の大部分および神奈川県北東部にあたる。

In a village in Musashi Province there lived two woodcutters, Mosaku and Minokichi. Mosaku was an old man and Minokichi, his young helper, was eighteen years old.

Every day they went together to a forest about five miles from their village. On the way to that forest there was a wide river to cross, and a boat to cross it.

Several bridges were built in the past but the bridges were always destroyed by floods. No bridge was strong enough to stand the high water.

Mosaku and Minokichi were coming home one very cold evening when a snowstorm suddenly struck. They reached the place where the boat was kept, but found that the boatman was gone and the boat was across the river.

They decided to stay in the boatman's house during the storm. It was a very small house with no fireplace and no window. The two men closed the door and lay down to rest on the *tatami*. They thought the storm would soon be over.

The old man fell asleep quickly, but Minokichi stayed awake listening to the awful wind and the roaring river. It was a terrible storm and the air became colder and colder. Later, he too fell asleep.

He was awakened by snow in his face. The door of the small house was open.

In the darkness he could see a woman dressed in white inside the room. She was standing above Mosaku and blowing her breath on him. Her breath was like white smoke.

Then she turned to Minokichi and bent over him. He tried to cry out but could not make a sound. Her face was almost touching his and he saw that she was very beautiful. But her cold eyes made him afraid.

She looked at him, then she smiled and whispered, "I was going to treat you like the other man. But I feel pity for you because you are so young. You are a pretty boy, Minokichi, and I will not hurt you now. But, if you ever tell anybody—even your own mother—about what you have seen tonight, I will know it. Then I will kill you. Remember what I say!"

She then turned and went out the door. He jumped up and looked out, but the woman was not there.

It was dark and the snow was coming into the small house. Minokichi closed the door tightly. He wondered if the wind had opened the door and if there really had been a white woman there.

He called Mosaku's name but the old man didn't answer. Minokichi became afraid. He reached over to touch Mosaku's face and found that it was as cold as ice. Mosaku was dead.

By morning the storm was over. When the boatman returned to his little station he found Minokichi lying senseless next to the frozen body of Mosaku.

Minokichi was cared for and became healthy again, but he was badly frightened by that terrible night. He said nothing about the woman in white.

Minokichi would return to the forest every morning to cut wood. He came home by evening with the wood. His mother helped him sell the wood.

One evening, the following winter, he met a girl traveling home on the same road. She was a tall, thin girl, very good-looking. She had a lovely voice, too.

He walked beside her and they began to talk. The girl said her name was O-Yuki. Both her parents had died recently and she was going to Yedo to find family to help her.

Minokichi soon felt charmed by this girl. He asked her if she was to be married and she answered, laughing, that she was free. Then she asked Minokichi if he was going to be married. He said he took care of his widowed mother and that they hadn't talked yet about marriage.

They walked on for a long time without speaking, but they were thinking about one another. By the time they reached the village, they were both feeling very happy.

Minokichi asked O-Yuki to rest awhile at his house. She decided to accept his offer. His mother made her feel welcome and prepared a warm meal for her.

Minokichi's mother also liked O-Yuki and suggested she delay her journey to Yedo. Well, Yuki never went to Yedo. She stayed in the house as the "honorable daughter-in-law."

O-Yuki was a good daughter-in-law. Five years later, when Minokichi's mother was dying, her last words were kind words of praise for the wife of her son.

O-Yuki and Minokichi had ten children, boys and girls. All of them were handsome children, very fair of skin.

The country people thought O-Yuki was a

wonderful person, though she was naturally different from them. Most country women age early in life, but even after having ten children she still looked young and fresh.

One night, after the children were asleep, O-Yuki was sewing by the light of a paper lamp.

Minokichi, watching her, said, "Seeing your face now reminds me of a strange thing that happened when I was a boy of eighteen. I saw somebody beautiful and white as you are now. She was very much like you."

Without lifting her eyes from her work, O-Yuki answered, "Tell me about her. Where did you see her?"

Then Minokichi told her about the terrible night in the boatman's small house; about the White Woman who bent over him then smiled and whispered; and about the silent death of Mosaku.

And he said, "Asleep or awake, that was the only time I've seen anyone as beautiful as you. Of course, she wasn't a human being, and I was very much afraid of her. But she was so white! I have never been sure if this Snow Woman was real or if I was dreaming."

O-Yuki threw down her sewing and stood above Minokichi.

She screamed into his face, "It was I   I   I —! I was that woman! I told you then that I would kill you if you ever said one word about it! I would kill you now if it weren't for the children. And now you had better take good care of them. For if they are ever unhappy with you, I will kill you."

She screamed and her voice became thin like a crying wind. She then changed into a bright white fog that rose to the roof and went out through the smoke-hole. She was never seen again.

Rokuro-Kubi

読みはじめる前に

Rokuro-Kubi
ろくろ首

　Rokuro-Kubi で使われている用語です。わからない語は巻末のワードリストで確認しましょう。

☐ brave　　　　☐ grasp　　　　☐ restore
☐ cruel　　　　☐ hairy　　　　☐ robber
☐ glory　　　　☐ loyal　　　　☐ soldier

●ろくろ首伝説

日本で有名な妖怪ろくろ首には2つのタイプがいる。1つは、お化け屋敷や幽霊話でおなじみの、首が長く伸びるもの。そしてもう1つが、中国の妖怪「飛頭蛮」に由来するともいわれる、首が抜けて頭が飛び回るものだ。本作品には、この「抜け首」ともいわれるろくろ首が登場する。

●主な登場人物と作品の舞台

Kwairyo　回龍　諸国を行脚する僧（雲水の旅客）。もとは磯貝平太左衛門武連という名の侍だった。

woodcutter　きこり　草むらで眠ろうとする回龍に、一夜の宿を提供する。

Kai　甲斐　旧国名のひとつ。現在の山梨県にあたる。

About five hundred years ago there lived a samurai named Isogai Heidazaemon Taketsura. He was in the service of Lord Kikuji of Kyushu.

He was a naturally brave and strong soldier. Even when as a boy he was as good as his teachers with a sword or a bow. Later, in the time of the Eikyo war, he received many high honors.

But when the House of Kikuji came to ruin, Isogai had no master. He could have worked for another *daimyo*, but he was still loyal to his former master.

Also he was not in search of glory. So he decided to cut his hair, and become a traveling priest. He took the Buddhist name of Kwairyo.

Kwairyo's heart was still the heart of a samurai. He was not afraid of danger. In all weather and all seasons he went places other priests didn't dare go. There was a lot of danger and fighting in those days. People on the road, including priests alone, were not safe.

During his first long journey, Kwairyo came to the province of Kai. One evening he was traveling through the mountains there. He was far from any village. It became dark. He decided to spend the night under the stars.

He was comfortable sleeping anywhere, in any weather. His body was as hard as iron. He found some grass near the road and lay down to sleep.

Soon, a woodcutter came along the road. He was surprised to see the priest lying down, and said, "Sir, don't you know that this is a dangerous place to sleep alone? Aren't you afraid of Hairy Things?"

"My friend," answered Kwairyo, "I am only a traveling priest, an *unsui-no-ryokaku*. I am not afraid of Hairy Things or creatures like that. I like lonely places. They are good for deep thinking. I am used to sleeping outside and am not worried about my life."

"You must be a brave man, Sir Priest, to lie down here!" the man said. "There is danger everywhere. Won't you please come to my small house for night? I have no food, but there is a roof over my head and you can sleep peacefully."

Kwairyo liked the man's kindness and accepted his offer. He followed the woodcutter along a narrow path through the mountain forest. It was a rough and dangerous path with many rocks and tree roots.

At last they came to a small clearing at the top of the hill. The moon was shining brightly. Kwairyo saw a small mountain cottage with a happy light burning inside.

The woodcutter took him to the small stream behind the house so they could wash their feet and hands. There was a vegetable garden nearby, and some pretty trees. In the distance was a waterfall, lighted by the moon.

Kwairyo entered the cottage with the

woodcutter. There were four people, men and women, sitting around the fire warming their hands. They bowed low to the priest in a manner of great respect.

"They are poor," thought Kwairyo, "but they are good people." Then he turned to the woodcutter, who was the master of the house, and said, "You are kind and polite. I imagine that you have not always been a woodcutter. Did you once belong to the upper classes?"

Smiling, the house-master answered, "Sir, you are correct. I was once a rather famous person. My story is the story of a ruined life. It was my own fault. I used to be a person of high rank in the service of a *daimyo*. But I loved women and wine too much. I became selfish and cruel. I brought ruin to my lord and caused the death of many people. I had to hide to save my life. Now I often pray to be forgiven, and I hope to restore our noble house. I try to do good things and to help people who are unlucky."

Kwairyo was pleased by this man's good heart. He said, "My friend, I have seen that mistakes made in youth can often be corrected in later years. In the Buddhist faith it is written that the power of doing wrong can be used to do right as well. I believe that you are a good man and that good fortune will come to you. Tonight I will pray that you receive the power to overcome past mistakes."

Kwairyo was then shown to a small side-room where a bed was prepared for him. When the others slept the priest stayed awake to read and pray for a long time. He looked through the window at the pretty scene outside before lying down.

The night was beautiful. The air was clear and fresh, the moon was bright. There was no wind. He could hear the musical sound of insects and the water in the stream.

He felt thirsty and decided to go outside for a drink. Slowly, quietly, he opened the sliding door to leave. In the light of the fire he saw the bodies of five people sleeping. Suddenly, he looked again—they had no heads!

For an instant he couldn't believe what he saw. He imagined a terrible crime. But then he realized there was no blood.

He thought, "Either these are ghosts, or I am in the home of *Rokuro-Kubi*. In the book of *Soshinki* it is written that *Rokuro-Kubi* are very evil. If one finds the headless body of a *Rokuro-Kubi*, and moves the body to another place, the head will never be able to join the body again. It also says that when the head returns and can't find its body, it will drop to the floor three times in great fear, then die. If these are *Rokuro-Kubi*, then I must do what the book tells me."

He picked up the house-master's body and pushed it out the window. Since the doors were locked, he guessed that the heads had gone out through the smoke-hole in the roof.

He gently unlocked the door, then walked quietly out through the garden into the group of trees. He heard voices talking. Quickly he walked from tree to tree, hiding in the shadows. From behind a large tree he could see five heads moving about and talking.

They were eating insects. At one point the house-master's head stopped eating and said, "Ah, I can't wait to eat the body of the traveling priest. Our stomachs will be full after tonight. I was foolish to talk to him because now he is praying for me. We can't touch him as long as he is awake and praying. But when he has gone to sleep.... One of you go to the house and see what he is doing."

The head of a young woman went towards the house and returned a minute later. She cried out, "That traveling priest is not in the house. He's gone! And he has taken the house-master's body! I don't know where it is."

When it heard this the house-master's head became very afraid. Its eyes opened wide, its hair stood up, and a loud cry came from its mouth.

Then with great anger it exclaimed, "If I cannot find my body then I must die! The priest has killed me! Before I die I will get him! I will tear him apart and eat him! Look, there he is—hiding behind that tree! Let's get him!!"

At that moment all five heads rushed towards Kwairyo. But the priest had picked up a tree branch to protect himself.

He struck the heads as hard as he could. Four of them went into the trees, but the house-master's head came back again and again. The mouth grasped onto the robe.

Kwairyo hit it many times until finally the head made a low sound and died. However, Kwairyo could not remove it from the robe.

The head was still hanging onto the robe when Kwairyo returned to the house. He saw the other four *Rokuro-Kubi*.

Their bloody heads were rejoined to their bodies and they were crying in pain. But when they saw him they all screamed, "The priest! The priest!" and ran out of the house into the forest.

The sky was beginning to brighten. Kwairyo knew they had power only at night.

He looked at the bloody, dirty, head on his robe and laughed to himself, "What a *miyage*!"

Then he gathered his belongings and walked down the mountain to continue his journey.

Later he came to Suwa in Shinano. He walked down the main street with the head at his elbow. Women fainted and children screamed. Soon a crowd gathered around him and the police came.

They took him to prison because they thought he had murdered someone and cut off his head. Kwairyo only smiled and said nothing.

The next day he was brought to the district court. He was ordered to explain how he, a priest, was walking around their town with a head on his robe.

Kwairyo laughed long and loudly at these questions. Then he said, "Sirs, I did not put the head there. It is holding on by itself. I have done no wrong. This is not the head of a man; it is the head of a ghost."

He then told the court the entire story of his adventure. He couldn't stop laughing when he talked about the five heads.

But the men of the court were not laughing. They judged him to be a criminal, not a priest. They then decided to have him killed immediately.

However, there was one old man who had remained silent during the trial. After hearing the opinion of the others, he spoke out. "I believe we must first examine the head to learn the truth. Please bring it here!"

The head was brought to the table with Kwairyo's robe still in its mouth.

The old man turned it around and around. He looked at it closely. He then showed the others several strange red marks on the neck. He also showed them that the head did not seem to be cut by any knife. In fact, the edges of the neck were very smooth.

He then said, "I am quite sure that the priest told us the truth. This is the head of a *Rokuro-Kubi*. These creatures always have red marks on the neck. Also, it is known that these ghosts have lived in the mountains of Kai from very ancient times. But you, Sir," he said, looking at Kwairyo, "you are a very different sort of priest. Why is it that you seem more like a soldier than a priest? Were you once a samurai?"

"You are correct, Sir," answered Kwairyo. "Before I was a priest I was a soldier for a long time. I had no fear of man or devil. My name then was Isogai Heidazaemon Taketsura, of Kyushu."

Many people in the room recognized and admired that name.

Kwairyo was now among friends, not judges. They brought him with honor to the palace of the *daimyo*. He was welcomed with a great feast.

Then, before he left Suwa he was given a nice gift. He was a very happy priest. He took the head with him, joking that he wanted it for a *miyage*.

Now, only the story of the head remains to be told.

A day or two after he left Suwa, Kwairyo met with a robber on the road. The robber made him take off his robe. That is when the robber saw the head hanging from the robe.

He dropped the cloth and jumped back, crying out, "What kind of priest are you!? You are worse than me. It is true that I have killed people, but I've never walked around with their heads. Well, Sir Priest, perhaps you and I are the same. I admire you! In fact, I would like that head and that robe to frighten people. Will you sell it? I will give you my robe and five *ryo* for the head."

Kwairyo answered, "I will let you have the robe and the head. But I must tell you that it is the head of a ghost, not a man. So if you buy it and have any trouble, please remember that I warned you."

"What a nice priest you are!" exclaimed the robber. "You kill men and then joke about it! But I am serious. Here is my robe and here is the money. Now give me the head."

"Take it," said Kwairyo. "But I'm not joking. You are a fool to pay for the head of a ghost." And Kwairyo, loudly laughing, walked away.

For a while the robber used the head to frighten people. He would frighten them and take their money. But when he arrived in Suwa one day, he learned the real history of the head.

Then he became afraid that the spirit of the *Rokuro-Kubi* might hurt him. So he decided to take the head back to the place it had come from.

He went to the little mountain cottage in Kai, but no one was there and he could not find the body. So he buried the head in the ground behind the house. Then he made a small grave of stone for the *Rokuro-Kubi*.

They say that the grave is still there today.

Mujina

Mujina
むじな

Mujina で使われている用語です。わからない語は巻末のワードリストで確認しましょう。

- ☐ ancient
- ☐ gently
- ☐ roughly
- ☐ bitterly
- ☐ merchant
- ☐ scream
- ☐ exclaim
- ☐ moat
- ☐ smooth

●主な登場人物と作品の舞台

old merchant　老年の商人　「むじな」に化かされたという人物。

O-jochu　お女中　紀伊国坂の道端でうずくまって泣いていたところを商人に発見される。

soba-seller　そば売り　紀伊国坂を登ったところでそば屋の屋台を構えていた。

Kiinokunizaka　紀伊国坂　現在の港区・外堀通りを四谷方面に上る坂道。

●現在の紀伊国坂

「むじな」が出て、人を化かすといわれた「紀伊国坂」。現在の港区赤坂にあるこの坂は、舗装され、その上を高速道路が通ってしまったこともあり、当時の面影を残すものは無くなってしまっているが、坂の下には「紀伊国坂」と書かれた標識が立っており、往時をしのばせている。

On the Akasaka Road in Tokyo there is a small hill called Kiinokunizaka. I don't know why it has this name. On one side of this hill there is an ancient moat, wide and deep. On the other side there are the long high walls of the palace. Before there were street lights and *jinrikishas*, this area was dark and lonely. Few people came here after dark because a Mujina used to walk there.

The last man to see the Mujina was an old merchant of Kyobashi. The merchant died about thirty years ago. This is the story he told:

One night, very late, he was hurrying up Kiinokunizaka when he saw a woman standing near the moat. She was all alone and weeping bitterly. He was afraid she might jump in the moat to kill herself, so he stopped to help her. She was a thin, well-dressed young lady.

"*O-jochu*," he exclaimed. "*O-jochu*, don't cry like that! Tell me your problem. Maybe I can help you." But she turned away from him, covered her face with her hands and continued to cry.

"*O-jochu*, please listen to me. This is no place for a young lady. Why are you crying?" He put his hand gently on her shoulder and said, "*O-jochu*! *O-jochu*! *O-jochu*! Listen to me for a moment. *O-jochu*! *O-jochu*!"

At that moment *O-jochu* turned around and took her hands away from her face. The man saw that she had no eyes or nose or mouth. He screamed and ran away.

He ran up Kiinokunizaka. He was too afraid to look back. At last he saw a distant light and ran towards it. It was the small shop of a *soba*-seller. When he got there he dropped to his knees and cried out, "Aa! aa! aa!!!"

"Hey! Hey!" exclaimed the *soba*-seller roughly. "What's wrong with you? Are you hurt?"

"No, I'm not hurt. It's just that.... Aa! aa!

46

I saw a woman, by the moat," explained the frightened man. "She showed me her.... Aa! I can't even tell you what I saw!"

"Well, did you see something like this?" cried the *soba*-seller, touching his own face. At that instant his face became smooth like an egg—and the light went out.

The Story of
Aoyagi

The Story of Aoyagi
青柳の話

The Story of Aoyagi で使われている用語です。わからない語は巻末のワードリストで確認しましょう。

☐ court   ☐ likeable   ☐ recite

☐ district   ☐ meantime   ☐ region

☐ lack   ☐ offer   ☐ soldier

●主な登場人物と作品の舞台

Tomotada 友忠 若い侍。京都への旅の途中、吹雪に遭い、山中の一軒家に泊めてもらうことになる。

Aoyagi 青柳 友忠が泊めてもらった一軒家にいた娘。美しく、教養がある。

Hatakeyama Yoshimune 畠山義統 友忠が使える能登の領主。

Hosokawa Masamoto 細川政元 友忠が使者に向かった京都の大名。

Noto 能登 旧国名の一つ。現在の石川県の一部にあたる地方。

　本文中に登場する短歌、漢詩について以下に元となったと
思われる日本語を併記して掲載する。

Tadzunetsuru,   尋ねつる
Hana ka tote koso,   花かとてこそ
Hı wo kurase,   日を暮せ
Akenu ni otoru   明けぬにおとる
Akane sasuran?   あかねすらん

Izuru hi no,   出ずる日の
Honomeku iro wo,   ほのめく色を
Waga sode ni,   わが袖に
Tsutsumaba asu mo, つつまば明日も
Kimiya tomaran.   君やとまらん

Koshi o-son gojin wo ou;   公子王孫　後塵を追う
Ryokuju namida wo tarete 緑珠 涙を垂れて
  rakin wo hitataru;   羅巾を滴る
Komon hitotabi irite   侯門 一たび入りて
  fukaki koto umi no gotoshi; 深きこと海のごとし
Kore yori shoro kore rojin. これより蕭郎 これ路人

In the time of Bummei there was a young samurai called Tomotada. He was in the service of Hatakeyama Yoshimune, the Lord of Noto.

Tomotada was from Echizen, but at an early age he was taken to study in the palace of the *daimyo* of Noto. He was educated there and trained as a soldier.

He was both a good student and a good samurai. He had a fine and likeable character, was quite good-looking, and was admired by many.

When Tomotada was about twenty years old he was sent on special duty to Hosokawa Masamoto, the great *daimyo* of Kyoto. The journey there passed through Echizen, so Tomotada asked to visit his widowed mother along the way.

It was the coldest time of the year when he

started. There was snow everywhere and he had to go slowly on his horse. The road took him through a mountain district where there were few villages.

On the second day of his difficult journey he could not reach the planned stopping place. He was worried because of strong winds and a coming snowstorm. The horse was very tired, too.

Then Tomotada spotted the roof of a small cottage at the top of a nearby hill. He managed to bring his horse to the cottage and he knocked loudly on the door.

An old woman opened it and saw the handsome young stranger. She kindly invited him inside.

Inside, Tomotada saw an old man and a girl sitting warming their hands around the warm fire. They asked him to join them. Then they prepared food and rice wine while they talked to the stranger.

Tomotada noticed that the young girl was

beautiful. However, her clothes were very old and dirty, and her long hair was uncombed. He wondered why such a pretty girl was living in such a place.

The old man said to him, "Honored sir, the next village is far, the snow and wind are strong. It is dangerous to continue. Although this cottage is not very nice, it is at least safe. We can take care of you and your horse tonight."

Tomotada accepted this kind offer. He was also secretly glad to see more of the young girl. She came in from the next room to serve the wine. She had changed her clothes and combed her hair. He gazed at her as she served him.

Tomotada thought she was now the most beautiful girl he had ever seen.

But the older woman said to him, "Sir, our daughter, Aoyagi, was born and raised here in the mountains. She knows nothing of gentle and polite service. Please pardon her manners."

Tomotada answered that he felt lucky to be in

the presence of such beauty. He could not take his eyes off her, which made her feel very shy. He didn't eat his food or drink his wine.

The mother said, "We hope you will eat our humble food. It is good for you." Then, to please the parents, he ate and drank.

But he could only think of the girl. He talked with her and found her speech to be as sweet as her face.

Though she was raised in the mountains, he believed her parents were educated people. She moved and spoke like a palace lady.

Suddenly, because of the happiness in his heart, he began to recite a poem:

> "*Tadzunetsuru,*
> *Hana ka tote koso,*
> *Hi wo kurase,*
> *Akenu ni otoru*
> *Akane sasuran?*"

("On my way to pay a visit, I found what I thought was a flower; therefore here I spend the day. Why in the time before dawn, the day's light should glow—that I don't know.")

Without waiting a moment, she answered him with a poem:

> "*Izuru hi no,*
> *Honomeku iro wo,*
> *Waga sode ni,*
> *Tsutsumaba asu mo,*
> *Kimiya tomaran.*"

("If with my robe I hide the faint fair color of the dawning sun, then perhaps in the morning my lord will remain.")

Tomotada then knew that she accepted his feelings for her. He was delighted by the art of her poetry and its message.

He was sure he would never meet another girl more beautiful or brighter than this girl. A voice inside him seemed to cry out, 'Take the luck that the gods have put before you!' He was completely taken by her.

He immediately asked the parents if he could marry their daughter. He also told them his name, his family and his position with the Lord of Noto.

They bowed low with respect, and great surprise at his request. But some moments later the father spoke to him.

"Honored master, you are a person of high position with a great future. We are grateful for what you ask of us. But our girl is a simple country girl. She has no training or teaching and it would not be right for her to marry a noble samurai. However, you seem to like the girl very much. You don't seem to care that she lacks manners. Therefore, we gladly present her to you as a humble maid."

The storm passed during the night and the cloudless morning arrived. Tomotada knew he had to leave, but he didn't want to leave the girl.

He then said to her parents, "I thank you for offering your daughter as my maid. However, I would like her to be my wife. Then, if you permit, I may take her with me as she is. I shall always be grateful to you as parents. In the meantime, please accept this humble gift for your kindness."

He then gave them a small quantity of gold *ryo*. But the old man, after bowing many times, gently pushed the gift back.

He said, "Kind master, the gold would be of no use to us. You will probably need it during your long journey. Here we buy nothing, and we could not spend so much money. We offer you our daughter for nothing, and you don't need to ask us to take her away. She told us already that she wants to go with you and stay with you as long as you want. We are getting old and it is time for us to separate. So we are lucky that you are able to take her now."

Tomotada tried to give money to the parents but they wouldn't take it. They were simply happy that he wanted to marry the girl. So he put her on his horse, and thanked her parents once again.

"Honored master," the father said, "it is we, not you, who have reason to be grateful. We know that you will be kind to our girl. Goodbye."

(Here, in the original Japanese story, there is a strange break in the story. There is no more mention of Aoyagi's parents or Tomotada's mother. It appears that Tomotada took Aoyagi with him to Kyoto and got into trouble. But we don't know where the couple lived later.)

…Now a samurai was not allowed to marry without permission from his lord. Tomotada could not get this permission before he returned from his special duty.

He was worried that Aoyagi's beauty might attract the dangerous attention of others. In Kyoto he tried to hide her from curious eyes.

But one day a servant of Lord Hosokawa saw Aoyagi. He learned of her relation to Tomotada and reported it to the *daimyo*. The *daimyo* was a young man who liked pretty faces. He ordered the girl to be brought to the palace.

Tomotada was terribly sad, but he knew there was nothing he could do, for now he was at the mercy of the powerful *daimyo*. Tomotada also knew that he was foolish to take the girl without asking his lord.

There was only one hope now—that Aoyagi might be able to escape from the palace and run away with him.

He decided to try to send her a letter. It would be dangerous, of course. If the *daimyo* discovered the letter Tomotada would be in serious trouble.

But he decided to try. He wrote a poem to her of only twenty-eight Chinese characters. But these characters said everything about his passion and loss.

> "*Koshi o-son gojin wo ou;*
> *Ryokuju namida wo tarete rakin wo hitataru;*
> *Komon hitotabi irite fukaki koto umi no gotoshi;*
> *Kore yori shoro kore rojin.*"

("Closely, the youthful prince now follows after the bright maid; the tears of the fair one fall and make her robes wet. But the lord has fallen deeply in love with her. Therefore it is only I that am sad and alone.")

The evening after this poem had been sent, Tomotada was ordered to appear before Lord Hosokawa. The young samurai was very afraid because he believed someone had told him about the letter.

'Now he will order my death,' thought Tomotada, 'but I don't care to live without Aoyagi. Besides, if I am to die I can at least try to kill Hosokawa.'

He put his swords into his robe and hurried to the palace.

He entered the meeting room and saw Lord Hosokawa surrounded by high-ranking samurai. He bowed many times. No one spoke, the silence was heavy and fearful.

But Hosokawa suddenly came down from his seat. He took the young samurai by the arm and began to repeat the words of the poem; "*Koshi o-son gojin wo ou.*" Tomotada looked up and was surprised to see a kind look in the prince's eyes.

Then Hosokawa said, "Because you love each other so much, I have decided to allow you to marry. We will have your wedding party here and now. The guests are all here, and the gifts are ready."

The prince gave a signal and the sliding doors opened. Tomotada saw many important people of the court. And there was Aoyagi in beautiful wedding clothes. Thus she was given back to him.

The wedding was joyous and wonderful. Expensive gifts were given to the young couple by the prince and others.

For five happy years Tomotada and Aoyagi lived together. But one morning they were talking together in their house. Aoyagi suddenly gave a cry of pain, then became very white and still.

After a few moments she said in a weak voice, "Pardon me for crying out. But the pain was so sudden! My dear husband, I think we met because of some karma in a former life. I also believe that we will meet again in a future life. But for now, our relation is now ending. We will be separated. Please repeat for me the *Nembutsu* prayer, because I am dying."

"Oh! What wild ideas you have!" cried her shocked husband. "Perhaps you are ill, my dear! Lie down for a while and rest; you will get better."

"No, no!" she answered. "I am dying. I'm sure of it! There is no need to hide the truth from you any longer. I am not a human being. The soul of a tree is my soul; the heart of a tree is my heart; the juice of the tree is my life. I am a willow tree. Someone at this cruel moment is cutting down my tree. That is why I must die! I have no strength to even weep. Quickly, repeat the *Nembutsu*. Quickly! Ah!"

With another cry of pain she tried to hide her beautiful face in her robe. But at the same moment her whole body began to fall in a strange way—down to the floor.

Tomotada tried to support her but there was nothing to support. On the floor lay her empty robes, but there was no body of the beautiful girl.

Tomotada cut off his hair and became a traveling Buddhist priest. He traveled through all the regions of the empire. In all the holy places he prayed for the soul of Aoyagi.

He arrived in Echizen during his journey and went to visit her parents. But when he came to the lonely place in the hills where they had lived he was very surprised.

The house had disappeared. There was nothing there except the stumps of three willow trees— two old ones and a young one—that had been cut down.

Next to these cut trees he built a memorial with holy words written on it. And he gave many Buddhist services to the spirits of Aoyagi and her parents.

A Dead Secret

A Dead Secret
葬られた秘密

A Dead Secret で使われている用語です。わからない語は巻末のワードリストで確認しましょう。

☐ contain ☐ movement ☐ secret
☐ drawer   ☐ possession ☐ spirit
☐ funeral   ☐ province   ☐ stare

●主な登場人物と作品の舞台

Inamuraya Gensuke 稲村屋源助　丹波の国の豪商。一人娘のお園を商人に嫁がせる。

O-Sono お園　「ながら屋」という商人のもとに嫁ぎ、子供も生まれたが、四年目に急死してしまう。

Daigen Osho 大玄和尚　お園の幽霊が出たことで相談を受け、「ながら屋」に赴く。

Tamba 丹波　旧国名のひとつ。現在の京都府北部地方にあたる。

A long time ago in the province of Tamba there lived a rich merchant named Inamuraya Gensuke. He had a daughter called O-Sono, who was very clever and pretty.

Inamuraya Gensuke wanted her to grow up with a better education than she could get in the country. So, he sent O-Sono to Kyoto to be trained by the ladies of the city.

After she was educated, she married a friend of the family, a merchant named Nagara-ya. She lived happily with him for nearly four years. They had one child, a boy. But O-Sono became ill and died in the fourth year of her marriage.

On the night after the funeral, O-Sono's little son said that his mama had come back. He said she was in the room upstairs, that she smiled but would not talk to him. Then some of the family went upstairs to O-Sono's room.

They were shocked to see the ghost-like figure of O-Sono. She appeared to be standing in front of a *tansu* which still contained her clothes. Her head and shoulders could be seen, but not the lower part of her body.

The people were afraid and left the room. They had a talk downstairs. The mother of O-Sono's husband said, "A woman likes her small, personal things. Perhaps O-Sono has come back to look at hers. Many dead people do that unless the things are given to the temple. If we give her clothes and things to the temple then her spirit will probably find rest."

They agreed to do this the following morning. All of O-Sono's possessions were taken to the temple. But she came back the next night, and again looked at the *tansu*. She also returned the following night, and every night thereafter. The house became a house of fear.

The mother of O-Sono's husband then went to the Zen temple to ask the priest for advice. The priest was a learned old man known as Daigen Osho. He said, "There must be something she is worried about in or near the *tansu*."

"But we took everything out!" replied the old woman.

"Well," said Daigen Osho, "tonight I shall go to your house to watch that room. Please tell the others that I must be alone in the room, unless I call for them."

After sundown Daigen Osho went to the house and to the room. He stayed there alone, praying. Nothing happened until after midnight, the hour of the rat. Then the figure of O-Sono suddenly appeared in front of the *tansu*. She kept watching it.

The priest spoke the holy words used in such cases. Then he talked to the figure of O-Sono. "I have come here to help you. Maybe there is something in that *tansu* that troubles you. Shall I try to find it for you?"

The shadowy figure appeared to agree. It

made a small movement with its head. The priest walked to the *tansu* and opened the top drawer. It was empty. So were the second, third, and fourth drawers.

He searched carefully between, behind and under them, but found nothing. However, the figure continued to stare with longing at the *tansu*. 'What can she want?' thought the priest.

Suddenly it occurred to him that there might be something under the paper which lined the drawers. He removed the paper of the first, second and third drawers, but found nothing.

Finally, under the paper in the bottom drawer he found a letter!

"Is this the thing that troubles you?" he asked. The shadow of O-Sono turned toward him. It was still looking at the letter.

"Shall I burn it for you?" he asked. She bowed before him.

"Then I shall burn it in the temple this morning," he promised, "and no one shall read it except me." The figure then smiled and disappeared.

The sun was just rising when the priest came down the stairs to the waiting family. "Don't worry," he said to them, "she will not come back again." And she never did.

The letter was burned. It was a love-letter written to O-Sono in the time of her studies at Kyoto. But only the priest knew what was in it; and the secret died when he later died.

The Dream of
Akinosuke

読みはじめる前に

The Dream of Akinosuke
安芸之介の夢

　The Dream of Akinosuke で使われている用語です。わか
らない語は巻末のワードリストで確認しましょう。

☐ ancient　　　☐ carriage　　　☐ official
☐ ant　　　　　☐ drag　　　　　☐ royal
☐ bride　　　　☐ governor　　　☐ servant

● 主な登場人物と作品の舞台

Miyata Akinosuke 宮田安芸之介　大和の十市に住む郷
　　士。

Kokuo of Tokoyo 常世の国王　安芸之介に自分の娘と
　　結婚するように言う。

Yamato Province 大和国　旧国名のひとつ。現在の奈良
　　県にあたる。

● 用語解説

goshi 郷士　封建時代に農業に従事していた武士。または
　　武士の待遇を受けていた農民。郷侍。

Tokoyo 常世の国　古代に、海の彼方にあると考えられて
　　いた国。また、転じて不老不死の仙境や黄泉の国を指す。

In the district of Toichi in Yamato Province there used to live a *goshi* named Miyata Akinosuke. In Akinosuke's garden there was a great, ancient cedar-tree. Akinosuke rested under the tree on hot days.

One very warm afternoon he was sitting under this tree drinking and talking with two other *goshis*. He suddenly felt very sleepy, so he lay down at the foot of the tree and dreamed this dream:

He saw a great line of people and carriages coming down the hill. It looked like the arrival of a great *daimyo*. He had never seen anything so grand, and it was coming towards his house.

He saw many young, well-dressed men carrying a beautiful palace-carriage. The large group arrived near the house and stopped.

A richly-dressed, important-looking man

walked over to Akinosuke and bowed deeply. He said, "Honored Sir, I am a servant of the *Kokuo* of Tokoyo. My master, the King, asks me to greet you and put myself at your service. He would also like you to come to the palace. Please get in this carriage and I will take you there."

Akinosuke was too surprised to answer. He got in the carriage. The servant then sat next to him and made a sign to the workers. The great carriage then began moving.

In a very short time the carriage stopped in front of a huge gate of Chinese style. Akinosuke had never seen it before. Here the servant got out, saying, "I will go announce your arrival."

After a little while Akinosuke saw two noble-looking men coming towards him. They were wearing robes of purple silk and tall hats. They helped Akinosuke get down from the carriage, then went through a great entrance and across a vast garden.

Akinosuke was shown to a beautiful waiting

room in the palace and he was seated in the place of honor. Serving maids brought food and drink.

The men in purple robes bowed to him and said, "It is now our duty to tell you why you are here. Our master, the King, wants you to marry his daughter. He wants you to marry the princess today. We shall soon take you to the room where the wedding will take place. The King is waiting there now. But first we must dress you in the proper clothes."

Several servants then walked with him to a great chest painted in gold. They opened it and took out many robes and other pieces of clothing.

Akinosuke soon looked like a royal person. He was taken to the wedding hall where he saw the *Kokuo* of Tokoyo sitting upon his great chair. He was wearing the black cap of state and was dressed in yellow silk robes.

Many important people sat next to him. They didn't move or speak. Akinosuke walked towards them and bowed to the King three times.

The King greeted him with kind words and said, "You know the reason why I have asked you to come here. We decided that you will be the husband of our only daughter—and the wedding will now take place."

As the King finished speaking, a sound of joyful music was heard. A long line of beautiful court ladies appeared from behind a curtain. They took Akinosuke to the room where the bride was waiting.

The room was huge and filled with wedding guests. They all bowed to Akinosuke as he entered and took his place facing the King's daughter. The princess was beautiful. Her clothes were beautiful too.

The marriage was performed with great happiness.

After the wedding, the pair was taken to a palace apartment that had been prepared for them. They received kind words from many noble people and too many gifts to count.

ceremony to wish him goodbye. Akinosuke was taken to the port. The ship sailed out into the blue sea under the blue sky. The island of Raishu gradually disappeared from view.

And Akinosuke suddenly woke up under the cedar-tree in his own garden.

For the moment he wasn't sure where he was. But he saw his two friends still sitting near him drinking and talking. He stared at them, then cried out, "How strange!"

"Akinosuke must have been dreaming," one of them said with a laugh. "What did you see that was strange, Akinosuke?"

Then Akinosuke told his dream about his twenty-three years on the island in the land of Tokoyo. They were really surprised because he had only been asleep for a few minutes.

One *goshi* said, "Indeed, you saw strange things. We also saw something strange while you were sleeping. A little yellow butterfly was flying above your face for a few seconds. We watched it land on the ground next to you. Then a big ant came out of a hole, seized the butterfly, and dragged it down into the hole. Just before you woke up the butterfly came out of the hole again. It flew over your face for a moment then suddenly disappeared. We don't know where it went."

"Perhaps it was Akinosuke's soul," said the other *goshi*. "I thought I saw it fly into his mouth. But if the butterfly was his soul it would not explain his dream."

"The ants might explain it," answered the first speaker. "Ants are strange creatures. Anyway, there is a big ant's nest under the cedar-tree."

"Let's look!" cried Akinosuke, as he went to find a tool to dig into the ground.

The ground below the cedar-tree had been dug up by the ants in a most amazing way. With grass and dirt they had built what looked like odd, tiny towns.

One of the little buildings was bigger than the rest. There were many ants moving quickly

around and through it. In the center of the building was a very large ant. It had yellow wings and a long black head.

"Why, there is the King of my dream!" cried Akinosuke. "There is the palace of Tokoyo! How amazing! Raishu should be somewhere to the southwest of it—near that big root. Yes, here it is! How very strange! Now I am sure I can find the mountain of Hanryoko where the princess is buried."

He searched and searched through the nest. At last he found the tiny hill. On the top of it was a tiny stone in the shape of a Buddhist memorial. Under it, in the dirt, he found the body of a female ant.

Diplomacy

Diplomacy
かけひき

Diplomacy で使われている用語です。わからない語は巻末のワードリストで確認しましょう。

☐ criminal   ☐ observe   ☐ spirit
☐ evil   ☐ pump   ☐ stepping-stone
☐ honor   ☐ revenge   ☐ sword

●用語解説

Karma 業 「業」とは「行為」のことであり、ヒンドゥー教および仏教ではその行為は功徳や罪障となって本人に返ってくると考えられている。また、前世の行為によって現世で受ける報い、転じて宿命や人が担う制約などを意味する。

segaki 施餓鬼 餓鬼道に落ちて飢餓に苦しむ無縁仏や生類のために食べ物を施し、その霊を供養する法会。浄土真宗以外の各宗派で、お盆の時期に行われるのが一般的。

A man was ordered to be killed in the garden of the *yashiki*. He was taken there and forced to get on his knees in the sand. His arms were tied behind him.

Servants brought in containers of water and bags filled with stones. These bags were placed all around the man so that he could not move. The master came to observe.

Suddenly, the man who was to die cried out to the master. "Honored Sir, what happened is not my fault. I am not a bad person or a criminal. I was very foolish, that's all. It was my Karma to be born foolish, and I can't help making mistakes. It is wrong to kill me for being a fool; it is evil. And that evil will come back to you. There will be revenge."

The samurai master knew about revenge. He knew that the angry spirit of someone who is killed would come back. It would come back to the killer.

He replied very gently, "You may try to frighten us after you are dead. But it is difficult to believe that you mean what you say. Will you try to show us your anger after your head has been cut off?"

"I certainly will," answered the man.

"Very well," said the samurai, taking out his long sword. "I am now going to cut off your head. Directly in front of you there is a stepping-stone. After your head has been cut off, try to bite the stepping-stone. If your angry spirit can help you do that, some of us may be frightened. Will you try to bite the stone?"

"I will bite it!" cried the man, in great anger, "I will bite it! I will bite..."

There was a flash of steel and a cutting sound. Blood from the headless man pumped into the air. The head rolled over the sand toward the stepping-stone. Then, suddenly, it caught the upper edge of the stone between its teeth, and held it tightly for a moment.

No one spoke, but the servants stared in terror at their master. He seemed unworried. He simply held out his sword so that a servant could pour water on it then wiped it clean with a soft cloth.

For many months after that day the workers and helpers lived in fear of angry spirits. They all believed that revenge would come.

They began to see and hear things which did not exist. They became afraid of the wind and the shadows. They had a meeting together and decided to have a *segaki* service performed to protect them.

"It's not necessary," said the samurai when he was told. "The desire of a dying man for revenge may be a cause for fear. But in this case there is nothing to fear."

The servant looked at his master curiously.

"Oh, the reason is very simple," declared the samurai. "Only the very last desire can be dangerous. But, I asked him to show me his anger in death by biting the stone. The last desire in his mind was to bite the stone, not the desire for revenge against us. He bit the stone and his revenge has been forgotten. You don't have to worry anymore about it."

And the dead man gave no more trouble. Nothing at all happened.

Word List

A

- □ **a lot of** たくさんの〜
- □ **a 〜 or two** 1〜か2〜、2, 3の
- □ **accept** 動 ①受け入れる ②同意する、認める
- □ **active** 形 ①活動的な ②積極的な ③活動［作動］中の
- □ **admire** 動 感心する、賞賛する
- □ **adventure** 名 冒険
- □ **advice** 名 忠告、助言、意見
- □ **affect** 動 ①影響する ②（病気などが）おかす
- □ **after that** その後
- □ **again and again** 何度も繰り返して
- □ **ah** 間《驚き・悲しみ・賞賛などを表して》ああ、やっぱり
- □ **Akamagaseki** 名 赤間が関《山口県下関市の旧名》
- □ **Akasaka** 名 赤坂《地名》
- □ **Akinosuke** 名 (宮田)安芸之介《人名》
- □ **all over** 全体に亘って、〜の至る所で
- □ **allow** 動 ①許す、《 – … to 〜》…が〜するのを可能にする、…に〜させて

おく ②与える
- □ **along** 熟 along the way 途中で come along ①一緒に来る、ついて来る ②やって来る、現れる ③うまくいく、よくなる、できあがる go along 〜に沿って行く
- □ **although** 接 〜だけれども、〜にもかかわらず、たとえ〜でも
- □ **always** 熟 not always 必ずしも〜であるとは限らない
- □ **amazing** 形 驚くべき、見事な
- □ **Amida-ji** 名 阿弥陀寺
- □ **ancient** 形 昔の、古代の
- □ **anger** 名 怒り
- □ **angrily** 副 怒って、腹立たしげに
- □ **announce** 動 （人に）知らせる、公表する
- □ **another** 熟 one another お互い
- □ **ant** 名 アリ（蟻）
- □ **Antoku Tenno** 安徳天皇（1178–1185）
- □ **anybody** 代 ①《疑問文・条件節で》誰か ②《否定文で》誰も（〜ない）③《肯定文で》誰でも
- □ **anymore** 副 《通例否定文、疑問文で》今はもう、これ以上、これから

92

□ **anyone** 代 ①《疑問文・条件節で》誰か ②《否定文で》誰も（～ない）③《肯定文で》誰でも

□ **anyway** 副 ①いずれにせよ，ともかく ②どんな方法でも

□ **anywhere** 副 どこかへ［に］，どこにも，どこへも，どこにでも

□ **Aoyagi** 名 青柳《人名》

□ **apart** 副 ばらばらに **tear apart** 引き裂く

□ **apartment** 名 アパート

□ **appear** 動 ①現れる，見えてくる ②（～のように）見える，～らしい **appear to** するように見える

□ **arm** 熟 **take someone by the arm**（人）の腕を捕らえる，腕をつかむ

□ **around** 熟 **move around** あちこち移動する **turn around** 振り向く，向きを変える，方向転換する **walk around** 歩き回る，ぶらぶら歩く

□ **arrival** 名 ①到着 ②到達

□ **art of** ～術

□ **artist** 名 芸術家

□ **as** 熟 **as good as** ～も同然で，ほとんど～ **as long as** ～する以上は，～である限りは **as much as** ～と同じだけ **as well** なお，その上，同様に **as ～ as one can** できる限り～ **as ～ as possible** できるだけ～ **be known as** ～として知られている

□ **ask ... if** ～かどうか…に尋ねる

□ **asleep** 形 眠って（いる状態の）**fall asleep** 眠り込む，寝入る

□ **at** 熟 **at last** ついに，とうとう **at least** 少なくとも **at once** すぐに，同時に **at peace** 平和に，安らかに，心穏やかで **at that moment** その時に，その瞬間に **at the foot of** ～のすそ［下部］に

□ **attention** 名 注意，集中

□ **attract** 動 引きつける，引く

□ **awake** 形 目が覚めて

□ **awaken** 動 目を覚まさせる，起こす，目覚める

□ **away** 熟 **go away** 立ち去る **run away** 走り去る，逃げ出す **take away** ①連れ去る ②取り上げる，奪い去る ③取り除く **take someone away**（人）を連れ出す **turn away** 向こうへ行く，追い払う，（顔を）そむける，横を向く **walk away** 立ち去る，遠ざかる

□ **awful** 形 ①ひどい，不愉快な ②恐ろしい

□ **awhile** 副 しばらくの間

B

□ **back** 熟 **come back** 戻る **come back to** ～へ帰ってくる，～に戻る **give back**（～を）返す **go back to** ～に帰る［戻る］**push back** 押し返す **take back** ①取り戻す ②（言葉，約束を）取り消す，撤回する

□ **badly** 副 ①悪く，まずく，へたに ②とても，ひどく

□ **battle** 名 戦闘，戦い

□ **battle of Dan-no-ura** 壇ノ浦の戦い《平安時代末期に現在の山口県下関市東方の壇ノ浦で行なわれた源平最後の海戦（1185）》

□ **beauty** 名 美，美しい人［物］

□ **because of** ～のために，～の理由で

□ **behind** 前 ①～の後ろに，～の背後に ②～に遅れて，～に劣って

□ **being** 名 存在，生命，人間 **human being** 人，人間

□ **belong**《－ to ～》～に属する，～のものである

□ **belongings**（持ち運びできる）持ち物，所有物

□ **below** 前 ①～より下に ②～以下の，～より劣る

☐ **bend over** かがむ, 腰をかがめる, ～に身をかがめる

☐ **bent** 動 bend (曲がる) の過去, 過去分詞

☐ **beside** 前 ①～のそばに, ～と並んで ②～と比べると ③～とはずれて

☐ **besides** 副 その上, さらに

☐ **better** 熟 even better さらに素晴らしいことに feel better 気分がよくなる get better (病気などが) 良くなる had better ～したほうが身のためだ, ～しなさい

☐ **bit** 動 bite (かむ) の過去, 過去分詞

☐ **bite** 動 かむ, かじる

☐ **bitter** 形 ①にがい ②つらい

☐ **bitterly** 副 激しく, 苦々しく

☐ **biwa** 名 琵琶

☐ **blame** 動 とがめる, 非難する

☐ **blind** 形 視覚障害がある, 目の不自由な

☐ **blood** 名 血, 血液

☐ **bloody** 形 血だらけの, 血なまぐさい, むごい

☐ **blow** 動 を吹く

☐ **board** 動 乗り込む

☐ **boatman** 名 (貸し) ボート屋, ボートの漕ぎ手, 船頭

☐ **both A and B** A も B も

☐ **bother** 動 悩ます, 困惑させる

☐ **bottom** 名 底, 下部, 最下位, 根底

☐ **bow** 名 弓 動 腰をかがめる, お辞儀をする

☐ **branch** 名 枝

☐ **brave** 形 勇敢な

☐ **breath** 名 息, 呼吸

☐ **breathe** 動 ①呼吸する ②ひと息つく, 休息する

☐ **bride** 名 花嫁, 新婦

☐ **brighten** 動 輝かせる, 快活にさせる

☐ **brightly** 副 明るく, 輝いて, 快活に

☐ **Buddhist** 形 仏教 (徒) の, 仏陀の 名 仏教徒

☐ **building** 名 建物, 建造物, ビルディング

☐ **Bummei** 名 文明年間《1469–1486》

☐ **bury** 動 埋葬する, 埋める

☐ **butterfly** 名 チョウ (蝶)

☐ **by oneself** 一人で, 自分だけで, 独力で

☐ **by the time** ～する時までに

C

☐ **call for** ～を求める, 訴える, ～を呼び求める, 呼び出す

☐ **call out** 叫ぶ, 呼び出す, 声を掛ける

☐ **call to** ～に声をかける

☐ **can** 熟 as ～ as one can できる限り～

☐ **cannot help ～ing** ～せずにはいられない

☐ **care** 熟 care for ～の世話をする, ～を扱う care to ～したいと思う take care of ～の世話をする, ～の面倒を見る take good care of ～を大事に扱う, 大切にする

☐ **carriage** 名 ①馬車 ②乗り物, 車

☐ **cedar-tree** 名 杉の木

☐ **ceremony** 名 儀式, 式典

☐ **certainly** 副 確かに, 必ず

☐ **character** 名 ①特性, 個性 ②文字, 記号 ④品性, 人格

☐ **charm** 動 魅了する

☐ **check** 動 ①照合する, 検査する ②阻止 [妨害] する ③ (所持品を) 預ける

☐ **chest** 名 ①大きな箱, 戸棚, たんす ②金庫

☐ **Chinese** 形 中国 (人) の 名 ①中国

人 ②中国語

- □ **clan** 名 ①氏族 ②一家, 一門
- □ **clear** 形 ①はっきりした, 明白な ②澄んだ
- □ **clearing** 名 (森林の)開拓地
- □ **clever** 形 ①頭のよい, 利口な ②器用な, 上手な
- □ **closely** 副 ①密接に ②念入りに, 詳しく ③ぴったりと
- □ **clothing** 名 衣類, 衣料品
- □ **cloudless** 形 雲のない
- □ **coast** 名 海岸, 沿岸
- □ **comb** 動 (髪を)くしですく
- □ **come** 熟 come along ①一緒に来る, ついて来る ②やって来る, 現れる ③うまくいく, よくなる, できあがる come back 戻る come back to ～へ帰ってくる, ～に戻る come down 下りて来る come in ～ from ～から来る come into ～に入ってくる come out of ～から出てくる come through 通り抜ける
- □ **comfortable** 形 快適な, 心地いい make oneself comfortable くつろぐ
- □ **coming** 形 今度の, 来たるべき
- □ **command** 動 命令する, 指揮する
- □ **completely** 副 完全に, すっかり
- □ **condition** 名 《-s》状況, 様子 social conditions 社会情勢
- □ **contain** 動 含む, 入っている
- □ **container** 名 容器, 入れ物
- □ **control** 動 ①管理[支配]する ②抑制する, コントロールする
- □ **correct** 形 正しい, 適切な, りっぱな 動 (誤りを)訂正する, 直す
- □ **cottage** 名 小別荘, 小さな家
- □ **could** 熟 If +《主語》+ could ～ できればなあ《仮定法》 could have done ～だったかもしれない《仮定法》
- □ **count** 動 数える

- □ **couple** 名 夫婦, 一組
- □ **course** 熟 of course もちろん, 当然
- □ **court** 名 宮廷, 宮殿
- □ **cover** 動 覆う, 包む, 隠す be covered with ～でおおわれている
- □ **crab** 名 カニ
- □ **creature** 名 (神の)創造物, 生物, 動物
- □ **crime** 名 ①(法律上の)罪, 犯罪 ②悪事, よくない行為
- □ **criminal** 名 犯罪者, 犯人
- □ **crowd** 名 群集
- □ **cruel** 形 残酷な, 厳しい
- □ **cry out** 叫ぶ
- □ **curious** 形 好奇心の強い, 珍しい, 奇妙な, 知りたがる
- □ **curiously** 副 ①不思議なことに ②もの珍しそうに
- □ **cut down** 切り倒す
- □ **cut off** 切断する, 切り離す
- □ **cutting** 形 身を切るような

D

- □ **Daigen Osho** 大玄和尚《人名》
- □ **daimyo** 名 大名
- □ **Dan-no-ura** 名 壇ノ浦《現在の山口県下関市》 battle of Dan-no-ura 壇ノ浦の戦い《平安時代末期に壇ノ浦で行なわれた源平最後の海戦(1185)》
- □ **dare** 動 思い切って[あえて]～する
- □ **darkness** 名 暗さ, 暗やみ
- □ **daughter-in-law** 名 義理の娘, (姑にとっての)嫁
- □ **dawn** 名 夜明け
- □ **dawning** 名 夜明け
- □ **day** 熟 in those days あのころは, 当時は one day (過去の)ある日, (未来の)いつか

95

□ **death** 名 死, 死ぬこと

□ **declare** 動 ①宣言する ②断言する

□ **deeply** 副 深く, 非常に

□ **delay** 動 遅らせる, 延期する

□ **delighted** 形 喜んでいる, うれしそうな

□ **demand** 動 要求する, 尋ねる

□ **desire** 名 欲望, 欲求, 願望

□ **destroy** 動 破壊する, 絶滅させる, 無効にする

□ **dig** 動 掘る **dig into** 掘り下げる **dig up** 掘り起こす, 掘り出す

□ **diplomacy** 名 外交, 外交的手腕

□ **directly** 副 ①じかに ②まっすぐに ③ちょうど

□ **dirt** 名 ①汚れ, 泥, ごみ ②土

□ **dirty** 形 汚い, 汚れた

□ **disappear** 動 見えなくなる, 姿を消す, なくなる

□ **distance** 名 距離, 隔たり, 遠方 **in the distance** 遠方に

□ **distant** 形 遠い, 隔たった

□ **district** 名 ①地方, 地域 ②行政区

□ **doorway** 名 戸口, 玄関, 出入り口

□ **down** 熟 **come down** 下りて来る **cut down** 切り倒す **get down** 降りる **lie down** 横たわる, 横になる **put down** 下に置く, 下ろす **throw down** 投げ出す, 放棄する

□ **downstairs** 副 階下で, 下の部屋で

□ **drag** 動 ①引きずる ②のろのろ動く[動かす]

□ **drawer** 名 引き出し

□ **dress in white** 白い服を着る

□ **drop to one's knees** がっくりと両ひざをつく

□ **dug** 動 dig (掘る) の過去, 過去分詞

□ **duty** 名 ①義務 (感), 責任 ②職務, 任務

□ **dying** 形 死にかかっている, 消えそうな

E

□ **each other** お互いに

□ **earless** 形 耳のない

□ **Echizen** 名 越前《地名》

□ **edge** 名 ①刃 ②端, 縁

□ **educate** 動 教育する, (～するように) 訓練する

□ **educated** 形 教養のある, 教育を受けた

□ **education** 名 教育, 教養

□ **Eikyo war** 永享の乱《室町幕府6代将軍足利義教による鎌倉公方足利持氏の討伐 (1438)》

□ **either A or B** AかそれともB

□ **elbow** 名 ひじ

□ **emperor** 名 天皇

□ **empire** 名 帝国

□ **entire** 形 全体の, 完全な, まったくの

□ **escape** 動 逃げる, 免れる

□ **even better** さらに素晴らしいことに

□ **ever since** それ以来ずっと

□ **everything** 代 すべてのこと[もの], 何でも, 何もかも

□ **everywhere** 副 どこにいても, いたるところに

□ **evil** 形 ①邪悪な ②有害な, 不吉な

□ **examine** 動 試験する, 調査[検査]する, 診察する

□ **except** 前 ～を除いて, ～のほかは

□ **exclaim** 動 ①(喜び・驚きなどで) 声をあげる ②声高に激しく言う

□ **exist** 動 存在する, 生存する, ある, いる

□ **expect** 動 予期[予測]する, (当然

のこととして）期待する

□ **eye** 熟 take one's eyes off ～から目をそらす

F

□ **fact** 熟 in fact つまり, 実は, 要するに

□ **faint** 形 かすかな, 弱い, ぼんやりした 動 気絶する

□ **fair** 形 ①正しい, 公平［正当］な ②色白の

□ **faith** 名 ①信念, 信仰 ②信頼, 信用

□ **fall asleep** 眠り込む, 寝入る

□ **fall in love with** ～に心を奪われる

□ **fallen** 動 fall（落ちる）の過去分詞

□ **famous for** 《be –》～で有名である

□ **far from** ～から遠い

□ **farming** 名 農業, 農作業

□ **fault** 名 過失, 誤り

□ **fear** 名 ①恐れ ②心配, 不安 in fear おどおどして, ビクビクして 動 ①恐れる ②心配する

□ **fearful** 形 恐ろしい

□ **feast** 名 饗宴

□ **feel better** 気分がよくなる

□ **feeling** 名 ①感じ, 気持ち

□ **feet** 熟 to one's feet 両足で立っている状態に

□ **female** 形 女性の, 婦人の, 雌の

□ **fighting** 名 戦闘

□ **figure** 名 人［物］の姿, 形

□ **filled with** 《be –》～でいっぱいになる

□ **fireplace** 名 暖炉

□ **fishermen** 名 fisherman（漁師）の複数形

□ **flash** 名 閃光, きらめき

□ **flood** 名 洪水

□ **fly over** 飛び超える

□ **fog** 名 濃霧

□ **following** 形 《the –》次の, 次に続く

□ **fool** 名 ばか者, おろかな人

□ **foolish** 形 おろかな, ばかばかしい

□ **foot** 熟 at the foot of ～のすそ［下部］に

□ **footstep** 名 足音, 歩み

□ **for a while** しばらくの間, 少しの間

□ **for nothing** ただで, 無料で

□ **for now** 今のところ, ひとまず

□ **for the moment** 差し当たり, 当座は

□ **force** 動 強制する, 力ずくで～する, 余儀なく～させる

□ **forgiven** 動 forgive（許す）の過去分詞

□ **former** 形 前の, 先の, 以前の

□ **fortune** 名 ①富, 財産 ②幸運, 繁栄, チャンス ③運命, 運勢

□ **friendly** 形 親しみのある, 親切な, 友情のこもった

□ **frighten** 動 驚かせる, びっくりさせる

□ **frightened** 形 おびえた, びっくりした

□ **front** 熟 in front of ～の前に, ～の正面に

□ **frozen** 形 凍った

□ **funeral** 名 葬式

G

□ **gather** 動 集まる, 集める

□ **gaze** 動 凝視する

□ **generously** 副 十分に, たっぷりと

A
B
C
D
E
F
G
H
I
J
K
L
M
N
O
P
Q
R
S
T
U
V
W
X
Y
Z

□ **Genji** 名源氏

□ **gentle** 形 ①優しい,温和な ②柔らかな

□ **gently** 副親切に,上品に,そっと,優しく

□ **get** 熟 get better (病気などが)良くなる get down 降りる get in 中に入る,乗り込む get into trouble 面倒を起こす,困った事になる,トラブルに巻き込まれる get on one's knees ひざまずく get out 外に出る,出て行く get there そこに到着する

□ **ghost** 名幽霊

□ **ghost-like** 形幽霊のような

□ **gift** 名贈り物

□ **give back** (〜を)返す

□ **glad to do** 《be –》〜してうれしい,喜んで〜する

□ **gladly** 副喜んで,うれしそうに

□ **glory** 名栄光,名誉,繁栄

□ **glow** 動 (火が)白熱して輝く

□ **go** 熟 go along 〜に沿って行く go away 立ち去る go back to 〜に帰る [戻る] go into 〜に入る go out 外出する,外へ出る,(火・明かりが)消える go through 通り抜ける go to sleep 寝る go without 〜なしですませる

□ **gold** 名金,金貨,金製品,金色

□ **good** 熟 as good as 〜も同然で,ほとんど〜 take good care of 〜を大事に扱う,大切にする

□ **good-looking** 形顔立ちのよい,ハンサムな,きれいな

□ **goshi** 名郷士

□ **govern** 動治める,管理する,支配する

□ **governor** 名 ①知事 ②支配者,(学校・病院・官庁などの)長

□ **gradually** 副だんだんと

□ **grand** 形雄大な,壮麗な

□ **grandchildren** 名 grandchild (孫)の複数

□ **grasp** 動つかむ,握る,とらえる

□ **grass** 名草

□ **grateful** 形感謝する,ありがたく思う

□ **grave** 名墓

□ **graveyard** 名墓地

□ **greet** 動 ①あいさつする ②(喜んで)迎える

□ **ground** 熟 on the ground 地面に

□ **grow up** 成長する,大人になる

□ **guard** 名 ①警戒,見張り ②番人 palace guard 衛兵

□ **guest** 名客,ゲスト

H

□ **had better** 〜したほうが身のためだ,〜しなさい

□ **hairy** 形毛むくじゃらの,毛製の Hairy Thing 魔物

□ **hall** 名公会堂,ホール,大広間,玄関

□ **handsome** 形端正な(顔立ちの),りっぱな,(男性が)ハンサムな

□ **hang** 動かかる,かける,つるす,ぶら下がる

□ **Hannya-Shin-Kyo** 名般若心経

□ **Hanryoko** 名盤龍岡《丘の名前》

□ **happen** 動起こる,生じる

□ **happily** 副幸福に,楽しく,うまく,幸いにも

□ **happiness** 名幸せ,喜び

□ **Hatakeyama Yoshimune** 畠山義統《能登の守護大名(?–1497)》

□ **haunt** 動よく行く,出没する,つきまとう

□ **have** 熟 could have done 〜だったかもしれない《仮定法》 have a talk 話をする should have done 〜すべきだった(のにしなかった)《仮

定法》

□ **headless** 形 頭部のない

□ **healthy** 形 健康な, 健全な, 健康によい

□ **hear of** ～について聞く

□ **Heike** 名 ①平家 ②平家の怨霊

□ **Heike crab** ヘイケガニ（平家蟹）

□ **help** 熟 cannot help ～ing ～せずにはいられない

□ **helper** 名 助手, 助けになるもの

□ **here and now** 今この場で

□ **here is ～** こちらは～です。

□ **hey** 間 ①《呼びかけ・注意を促して》おい, ちょっと ②へえ, おや, まあ

□ **hide** 動 隠れる, 隠す, 隠れて見えない, 秘密にする

□ **high-ranking** 形 地位［身分］の高い

□ **Hoichi** 名 芳一《人名》

□ **hold on** しっかりつかまる

□ **hold out** 差し出す, (腕を)伸ばす

□ **holy** 形 聖なる, 神聖な

□ **honor** 名 名誉, 光栄, 信用

□ **honorable** 形 ①尊敬すべき, 立派な ②名誉ある ③高貴な

□ **honored** 形 名誉ある, 光栄に思って

□ **Hosokawa Masamoto** 細川政元《室町時代の大名（1466–1507）》

□ **hour of the rat** 子 (ね) の刻（深夜十二時前後の時間帯）

□ **house-master** 名 家主, 家長

□ **however** 接 けれども, だが

□ **huge** 形 巨大な, ばく大な

□ **human being** 人, 人間

□ **humble** 形 つつましい, 粗末な

□ **hurry up** 急ぐ

I

□ **if** 熟 If +《主語》+ could ～できればなあ《仮定法》 **ask … if ～** ～かどうか…に尋ねる **wonder if ～** ではないかと思う

□ **imagine** 動 想像する, 心に思い描く

□ **immediately** 副 すぐに, ～するやいなや

□ **important-look** 形 重要（人物）に見える

□ **improve** 動 改善する［させる］, 進歩する

□ **in** 熟 **in fact** つまり, 実は, 要するに **in fear** おどおどして, ビクビクして **in front of** ～の前に, ～の正面に **in search of** ～を探し求めて **in the distance** 遠方に **in the meantime** それまでは, 当分は **in the presence of** ～の面前で **in the shape of** ～の形をした **in those days** あのころは, 当時は

□ **Inamuraya Gensuke** 稲村屋源助《人名》

□ **including** 前 ～を含めて, 込みで

□ **indeed** 副 本当に, まさか

□ **insect** 名 虫, 昆虫

□ **instant** 名 瞬間, 寸珍

□ **instead** 副 その代わりに

□ **interrupt** 動 さえぎる, 妨害する, 口をはさむ

□ **iron** 名 鉄, 鉄製のもの

□ **Isogai Heidazaemon Taketsura** 磯貝平太左衛門武連《人名》

□ **It is ～ for someone to …** (人)が…するのは～だ

□ **itself** 代 それ自体, それ自身

J

□ **Japanese** 形 日本 (人・語) の

□ **jinrikisha** 图人力車

□ **joke** 動冗談を言う, ふざける, からかう

□ **journey** 图①(遠い目的地への)旅 ②行程

□ **joyful** 形楽しませる, 喜びに満ちた

□ **joyous** 形うれしい, 喜びに満ちた

□ **judge** 動判決を下す, 裁く, 判断する 图裁判官, 判事, 審査員

□ **jump up** 素早く立ち上がる

K

□ **Kai** 图甲斐《地名》

□ **kaimon** 图開門

□ **karma** 图業(ごう), カルマ

□ **Kiinokunizaka** 图紀伊国坂《現在の東京都港区にある坂の名》

□ **Kikuji** 图菊池《人名》

□ **killer** 图殺人者[犯]

□ **kind of** ～のようなもの[人]

□ **kind to** 《be –》～に親切である

□ **kindly** 副親切に, 優しく

□ **kindness** 图親切(な行為), 優しさ

□ **knee** 图ひざ **drop to one's knees** がっくりと両ひざをつく **get on one's knees** ひざまずく

□ **knife** 图ナイフ, 小刀, 短剣

□ **knock** 動ノックする

□ **know nothing of** ～のことを知らない

□ **know of** ～について知っている

□ **known as** 《be –》～として知られている

□ **Kokuo of Tokoyo** 图常世の国王《人名》

□ **Kwairyo** 图回龍《人名》

□ **Kyobashi** 图京橋《地名》

□ **Kyoto** 图京都《地名》

□ **Kyushu** 图九州《地名》

L

□ **lack** 動不足している, 欠けている

□ **lamp** 图ランプ, 灯火

□ **last** **at last** ついに, とうとう

□ **later** 熟 **some time later** しばらくして

□ **lay** 動lie(横たわる)の過去

□ **least** 图最小, 最少 **at least** 少なくとも

□ **less** 形～より小さい[少ない] 副～より少なく, ～ほどでなく

□ **lie** 動横たわる, 寝る **lie down** 横たわる, 横になる

□ **lift** 動持ち上げる, 上がる

□ **like** 熟 **like this** このような, こんなふうに **look like** ～のように見える, ～に似ている **sound like** ～のように聞こえる **would like** ～がほしい **would like to** ～したいと思う

□ **likeable** 形好感の持てる, 魅力のある

□ **line of** ～の系統, 血筋

□ **listener** 图聞く人, ラジオ聴取者

□ **live** 熟 **there lived ～.** ～が住んでいました。

□ **lonely** 形①孤独な, 心さびしい ②ひっそりした, 人里離れた

□ **long** **as long as** ～する以上は, ～である限りは

□ **longer** 熟 **no longer** もはや～でない[～しない]

□ **longing** 形切望の

□ **look** 熟 **look in** 中を見る, 立ち寄る **look like** ～のように見える, ～に似ている **look out** 外を見る **look through** ～をのぞき込む **look up** 見上げる

- ☐ **lord** 图首長, 主人, 領主
- ☐ **lose sight of** ～を見失う
- ☐ **loss** 图①損失（額・物）, 損害, 浪費 ②失敗, 敗北
- ☐ **lot of** 《a－》たくさんの～
- ☐ **loudly** 副大声で, 騒がしく
- ☐ **love-letter** 图恋文
- ☐ **lovely** 形愛らしい, 美しい, すばらしい
- ☐ **lower** 形もっと低い
- ☐ **loyal** 形忠実な, 誠実な
- ☐ **lying** 動lie（横たわる）の現在分詞

M

- ☐ **maid** 图お手伝い, メイド
- ☐ **main** 形主な, 主要な
- ☐ **make a mistake** 間違いをする
- ☐ **make noise** 音を立てる
- ☐ **make oneself comfortable** くつろぐ
- ☐ **mama** 图ママ
- ☐ **manage** 動①動かす, うまく処理する ②どうにか～する
- ☐ **manner** 图①方法, やり方 ②態度, 様子 ③《-s》行儀, 作法, 生活様式
- ☐ **many** 熟so many 非常に多くの
- ☐ **mark** 图印, 記号, 跡
- ☐ **marriage** 图結婚（生活・式）
- ☐ **married** 形結婚した, 既婚の
- ☐ **marry** 動結婚する
- ☐ **master** 图主人, 雇い主, 師
- ☐ **mean what one say** 本気である
- ☐ **meantime** 图合間, その間 in the meantime それまでは, 当分は
- ☐ **meet with** ～に出会う
- ☐ **meeting** 图集まり, ミーティング

- ☐ **memorial** 图記念物, 記録
- ☐ **mention** 图言及, 陳述
- ☐ **merchant** 图商人, 貿易商
- ☐ **mercy** 图情け, 哀れみ, 慈悲
- ☐ **messenger** 图使者, 伝達者
- ☐ **midnight** 图夜の12時, 真夜中, 暗黒
- ☐ **might** 助《mayの過去》①～かもしれない ②～してもよい, ～できる
- ☐ **mile** 图マイル《長さの単位。1,609m》
- ☐ **Mimi-nashi-Hoichi** 图耳なし芳一《人名》
- ☐ **Minamoto** 图源《人名》
- ☐ **Minamoto clan** 源氏（一族）
- ☐ **mind** 图心, 精神, 考え
- ☐ **Minokichi** 图巳之吉《人名》
- ☐ **mistake** 熟make a mistake 間違いをする
- ☐ **miyage** 图土産
- ☐ **Miyata Akinosuke** 宮田安芸之介《人名》
- ☐ **moat** 图堀
- ☐ **moment** 图①瞬間, ちょっとの間 ②（特定の）時, 時期 at that moment その時に, その瞬間に for a moment 少しの間 for the moment 差し当たり, 当座は
- ☐ **more** 熟more of ～よりもっと more than ～以上 no more もう～ない
- ☐ **morning** 熟one morning ある朝
- ☐ **Mosaku** 图茂作《人名》
- ☐ **move about** 動き回る
- ☐ **move around** あちこち移動する
- ☐ **movement** 图動き, 運動
- ☐ **much** 熟as much as ～と同じだけ too much 過度の
- ☐ **Mujina** 图むじな《狢の異称。人を化かすと思われていた》

□ **murder** 動殺す

□ **Musashi Province** 武蔵国《地名》

□ **musical** 形音楽の

N

□ **Nagara-ya** 名ながら屋《商家の名》

□ **narrow** 形狭い

□ **naturally** 副生まれつき, 自然に, 当然

□ **nearby** 形近くの, 間近の 副近くで, 間近で

□ **nearly** 副ほとんど

□ **necessary** 形必要な, 必然の

□ **Nembutsu** 名念仏

□ **nest** 名巣

□ **no longer** もはや~でない [~しない]

□ **no more** もう~ない

□ **no one** 誰も [一人も]~ない

□ **no use** 《of-》使われないで

□ **noble** 形気高い, 高貴な, りっぱな, 高貴な 名貴族

□ **noble-looking** 形高貴な様子の, 身分が高そうに見える

□ **nobody** 代誰も [1人も]~ない

□ **noise** 名騒音, 騒ぎ, 物音 **make noise** 音を立てる

□ **not always** 必ずしも~であるとは限らない

□ **not yet** まだ~してない

□ **not ~ but ...** ~ではなくて…

□ **nothing** 熟 for nothing ただで, 無料で **know nothing of** ~のことを知らない

□ **notice** 動気づく, 認める

□ **Noto** 名能登《地名》

□ **now** 熟 for now 今のところ, ひと

まず **here and now** 今この場で

O

□ **obey** 動服従する, (命令などに) 従う

□ **observe** 動観察 [観測] する, 監視 [注視] する

□ **occur** 動 (事が) 起こる, 生じる, (考えなどが) 浮かぶ **occur to** ふと気が付く, ~の心に浮かぶ

□ **odd** 形奇妙な

□ **of course** もちろん, 当然

□ **of no use** 使われないで

□ **of one's own** 自分自身の

□ **off** 熟 cut off 切断する, 切り離す **take off** (衣服を) 脱ぐ, 取り去る, ~を取り除く **take one's eyes off** ~から目をそらす **tear off** 引きはがす

□ **offer** 動申し出る, 申し込む, 提供 名提案, 提供

□ **official** 動役人, 公務員

□ **O-jochu** 名お女中《若い女性への呼びかけの語》

□ **on one's way to** ~に行く途中で

□ **on the ground** 地面に

□ **on the way to** ~へ行く途中で

□ **once** 熟 at once すぐに, 同時に

□ **one** 熟 no one 誰も [一人も]~ない **one another** お互い **one day** (過去の) ある日, (未来の) いつか **one morning** ある朝

□ **Oni-bi** 名鬼火

□ **onto** 前~の上へ [に]

□ **original** 形始めの, 元の, 本来の

□ **Osho** 名和尚

□ **O-Sono** 名お園《人名》

□ **other** 熟 each other お互いに

□ **out** 熟 call out 叫ぶ, 呼び出す, 声

を掛ける **come out of** 〜から出て
くる **cry out** 叫ぶ **get out** 外に出る,
出て行く **go out** 外出する, 外へ出
る, (火・明かりが)消える **hold out**
差し出す, (腕を)伸ばす **look out** 外
を見る **out of** ①〜から外へ, 〜から
抜け出して ②〜から作り出して, 〜
を材料として ③〜の範囲外に, 〜か
ら離れて ④(ある数)の中から **push
out** 突き出す **speak out** はっきり
[遠慮なく]言う **take out** 取り出す,
取り外す, 連れ出す, 持って帰る

□ **over** 熟 **all over** 全体に亘って, 〜
の至る所で **be over** 終わる **bend
over** かがむ, 腰をかがめる, 〜に身を
かがめる **fly over** 飛び超える **reach
over** 手を伸ばす **walk over** 〜の方
に歩いていく

□ **overcome** 動 勝つ, 打ち勝つ, 克
服する

□ **overlook** 動 ①見落とす, (チャン
スなどを)逃す ②見渡す ③大目に見
る 名 見晴らし

□ **own** 熟 **of one's own** 自分自身の

□ **O-Yuki** 名 お雪《人名》

P

□ **pair** 名 (2つから成る)一対, 一組,
ペア

□ **palace** 名 宮殿, 大邸宅 **palace
guard** 衛兵

□ **palace-carriage** 名 宮廷の馬車
[御所車]

□ **parent** 名《-s》両親

□ **pass through** 〜を通る, 通行す
る

□ **passion** 名 情熱, (〜への)熱中,
激怒

□ **past** 形 過去の, この前の 名 過去(の
出来事) 副《時間・場所》〜を過ぎて,
〜を越して

□ **path** 名 ①(踏まれてできた)小道,
歩道 ②進路, 通路

□ **pay** 動 支払う, 払う, 報いる, 償う
pay a visit 〜を訪問する

□ **peace** 熟 **at peace** 平和に, 安らか
に, 心穏やかで

□ **peacefully** 副 平和に, 穏やかに

□ **perform** 動 (任務などを)行う, 果
たす, 実行する

□ **perhaps** 副 たぶん, ことによると

□ **permission** 名 許可, 免許

□ **permit** 動 許可する

□ **personal** 形 ①個人の, 私的な ②
本人自らの

□ **pick up** 拾い上げる

□ **pity** 名 哀れみ, 同情, 残念なこと

□ **place** 熟 **take one's place** (人と)
交代する, (人)の代わりをする, 後任
になる **take place** 行われる, 起こる

□ **player** 名 演奏者

□ **pleasant** 形 (物事が)楽しい, 心
地よい

□ **pleased** 形 喜んだ, 気に入った

□ **poetry** 名 詩歌

□ **polite** 形 ていねいな, 礼儀正しい,
洗練された

□ **pool** 名 水たまり, プール

□ **porch** 名 ポーチ, 玄関

□ **port** 名 港

□ **position** 名 地位, 身分

□ **possessed** 形 取りつかれた **be
possessed by** 〜にとらわれる

□ **possession** 名 ①所有(物) ②財
産, 領土

□ **possible** 形 ①可能な ②ありうる,
起こりうる **as 〜 as possible** でき
るだけ〜

□ **pour** 動 注ぐ, 浴びせる

□ **powerful** 形 力強い, 実力のある,
影響力のある

□ **praise** 名 賞賛

□ **pray for** 〜のために祈る

□ **prayer** 名 ①祈り, 祈願(文) ②祈る人

□ **prepare for** ～の準備をする

□ **prepared** 形 準備[用意]のできた

□ **presence** 名 ①存在すること ②出席, 態度 **in the presence of** ～の面前で

□ **priest** 名 和尚, 僧侶

□ **prince** 名 王子

□ **princess** 名 王女

□ **prison** 名 刑務所, 監獄

□ **private** 形 私的な, 個人の

□ **probably** たぶん, あるいは

□ **proper** 形 適した, 適切な, 正しい

□ **prove** 動 ①証明する ②(～である ことが)わかる, (～と)なる

□ **province** 名 ①州, 省 ②地方, 田舎

□ **pump** 動 (ドッと)流れる, ほとばしり出る

□ **purple** 形 紫色の

□ **push back** 押し返す

□ **push out** 突き出す

□ **put down** 下に置く, 下ろす

□ **put ～ on ...** ～を…の上に置く

□ **put ～ into ...** ～を…に突っ込む

Q

□ **quantity** 名 ①量 ②《-ties》多量, たくさん

□ **quickly** 副 敏速に, 急いで

□ **quietly** 副 ①静かに ②平穏に, 控えめに

R

□ **raise** 動 ～を育てる

□ **Raishu** 名 萊州《中国にかつて存在した州。現在の山東省煙台市一帯》

□ **rank** 名 階級, 位

□ **rat** 名 hour of the rat 子(ね)の刻 (深夜十二時前後の時間帯)

□ **rather** 副 ①むしろ, かえって ②かなり, いくぶん, やや

□ **reach over** 手を伸ばす

□ **realize** 動 理解する, 実現する

□ **recently** 副 近ごろ, 最近

□ **recite** 動 暗唱する, 復唱する, 物語る, 朗読する

□ **recognize** 動 認める, 認識[承認]する

□ **recover** 動 ①取り戻す, ばん回する ②回復する

□ **region** 名 ①地方, 地域 ②範囲

□ **rejoin** 動 復帰する, 再び一緒になる

□ **relation** 名 ①(利害)関係, 間柄 ②親戚

□ **remain** 動 ①残っている, 残る ② (～の)ままである[いる]

□ **remind** 動 思い出させる, 気づかせる

□ **remove** 動 取り去る, 除去する

□ **repeat** 動 繰り返す

□ **reply** 動 答える, 返事をする, 応答する

□ **request** 名 願い, 要求(物)

□ **respect** 名 ①尊敬, 尊重 ②注意, 考慮

□ **rest on** ～の上に載っている

□ **restore** 動 元に戻す, 復活させる

□ **revenge** 名 復讐

□ **reward** 動 報いる

□ **rice wine** 日本酒

□ **richly-dressed** 形 立派な服装をした

□ **roaring** 形 轟音を立てる

□ **robber** 名 泥棒, 強盗

WORD LIST

- **robe** 名ローブ, 法服, 式服
- **Rokuro-kubi** 名ろくろ首
- **roll** 動転がる, 転がす roll over 転がる
- **roof** 名屋根
- **root** 名根
- **rough** 形①(手触りが)粗い ②荒々しい, 未加工の
- **roughly** 副①おおよそ, 概略的に, 大ざっぱに ②手荒く, 粗雑に
- **royal** 形王の, 女王の, 国立の
- **ruin** 名破滅, 滅亡, 破産 動破滅させる
- **run away** 走り去る, 逃げ出す
- **run up** ～に走り寄る
- **rush** 動突進する
- **ryo** 名①両《お金の単位》②小判

S

- **sadness** 名悲しみ, 悲哀
- **sail** 動帆走する, 航海する, 出航する
- **samurai** 名侍
- **sand** 名砂
- **scream** 動叫ぶ, 金切り声を出す
- **search** 動捜し求める, 調べる 名捜査, 探索, 調査 in search of ～を探し求めて
- **secret** 名秘密, 神秘
- **secretly** 副秘密に, 内緒で
- **seem** 動(～に)見える, (～のように)思われる seem to be ～であるように思われる
- **segaki** 名施餓鬼《餓鬼道におちて飢餓に苦しむ亡者(餓鬼)に飲食物を施す意で, 無縁の亡者のために催す読経や供養》
- **seize** 動①ぐっとつかむ, 捕らえる ②襲う

- **selfish** 形わがままな, 自分本位の, 利己主義の
- **sense** 動感じる, 気づく
- **senseless** 形無感覚の, 無意識の
- **separate** 動①分ける, 分かれる, 隔てる ②別れる, 別れさせる
- **serious** 形①まじめな, 真剣な ②重大な, 深刻な, (病気などが)重い
- **servant** 名召使, 使用人, しもべ
- **serve** 動①仕える, 奉仕する ②(客の)応対をする, 給仕する, 食事[飲み物]を出す
- **service** 名①勤務, 業務 ②奉仕, 貢献
- **serving** 名給仕をすること
- **sewing** 名裁縫, 縫い物
- **shadow** 名影, 暗がり
- **shadowy** 形影のある, 陰の多い, 暗い, おぼろげな
- **Shall I ～?** (私が)～しましょうか。
- **shape** 名形, 姿, 型
- **shape** 熟in the shape of ～の形をした
- **Shimonoseki** 名下関《地名》
- **Shinano** 名信濃《地名》
- **shine** 動光る, 輝く
- **shocked** 形～にショックを受けて, 憤慨して
- **shore** 名岸, 海岸, 陸
- **should have done** ～すべきだった(のにしなかった)《仮定法》
- **shoulder** 名肩
- **shouting** 名叫び
- **shown** 動show(見せる)の過去分詞
- **shy** 形内気な, 恥ずかしがりの, 臆病な
- **side** 名側, 横, そば
- **side-room** 名横の部屋, わきの部屋

105

□ **sight** 熟 lose sight of 〜を見失う

□ **signal** 名 合図

□ **silence** 名 沈黙, 無言, 静寂

□ **silent** 形 ①無言の, 黙っている ②静かな, 音を立てない

□ **silk** 名 絹(布), 生糸 形 絹の, 絹製の

□ **simply** 副 ①簡単に ②単に, ただ ③まったく, 完全に

□ **since** 熟 ever since それ以来ずっと

□ **sing of** 〜のことを歌う

□ **singer** 名 歌手

□ **sink** 動 沈む, 沈める

□ **skill** 名 ①技能, 技術 ②上手, 熟練

□ **sleep** 熟 go to sleep 寝る

□ **sleepy** 形 ①眠い, 眠そうな ②活気のない

□ **sliding door** 引き戸

□ **slowly** 副 遅く, ゆっくり

□ **smoke** 名 煙, 煙状のもの

□ **smoke-hole** 名 煙出し

□ **smooth** 形 滑らかな, すべすべした

□ **snowstorm** 名 吹雪

□ **so many** 非常に多くの

□ **so that** 〜するために, それで, 〜できるように

□ **so 〜 that ...** 非常に〜なので…

□ **soba-seller** 名 そば売り

□ **social** 形 ①社会の, 社会的な ②社交的な, 愛想のよい social conditions 社会情勢

□ **soil** 名 土

□ **soldier** 名 兵士, 兵卒

□ **some time later** しばらくして

□ **somebody** 代 誰か, ある人

□ **someone** 代 ある人, 誰か

□ **something** 代 ①ある物, 何か ②いくぶん, 多少

□ **somewhere** 副 ①どこかへ[に] ②いつか, およそ

□ **sort** 名 種類, 品質 a sort of 〜のようなもの, 一種の〜

□ **Soshinki** 『捜神記』《東晋の干宝による志怪小説集》

□ **soul** 名 魂

□ **sound like** 〜のように聞こえる

□ **southwest** 名 南西(部)

□ **southwestern** 名 南西の, 南西向きの

□ **speak out** はっきり[遠慮なく]言う

□ **speaker** 名 話す人, 演説者, 代弁者

□ **spirit** 名 ①霊 ②精神, 気力

□ **spot** 動 〜を見つける

□ **stair** 名 《-s》階段, はしご

□ **stand up** 立ち上がる

□ **stare** 動 じっと[じろじろ]見る

□ **state** 名 階層, 地位

□ **stay in** 家にいる, (場所)に泊まる, 滞在する

□ **stay with** (人)と一緒に暮らす

□ **steel** 名 鋼, 鋼鉄(製の物)

□ **stepping-stone** 名 飛び石

□ **stomach** 名 ①胃, 腹 ②食欲, 欲望, 好み

□ **stone** 名 石, 小石

□ **stopping place** 立ち寄り場所

□ **storm** 名 嵐, 暴風雨

□ **story-telling** 名 ものを語ること

□ **stranger** 名 見知らぬ人, 他人

□ **stream** 名 小川, 流れ

□ **strength** 名 力, 体力

□ **struck** 動 strike (打つ)の過去, 過去分詞

□ **stump** 名 木の切り株

□ **style** 名 やり方, 流儀, 様式, スタイル

☐ **success** 名成功, 幸運, 上首尾

☐ **such a** そのような

☐ **such ~ that ...** 非常に~なので...

☐ **sudden** 形突然の, 急な

☐ **suggest** 動①提案する ②示唆する

☐ **sundown** 名日暮れ

☐ **sunrise** 名日の出

☐ **sunset** 名日没, 夕焼け

☐ **support** 動支える, 支持する

☐ **surprised** 形驚いた **be surprised at** ~に驚く

☐ **surround** 動囲む, 包囲する

☐ **Suwa** 名諏訪《地名》

☐ **swimmer** 名泳ぐ人

☐ **sword** 名剣, 刀

T

☐ **Taira clan** 平氏 (一族)

☐ **take** 熟 **take away** ①連れ去る ②取り上げる, 奪い去る ③取り除く **take back** ①取り戻す ②（言葉, 約束を）取り消す, 撤回する **take care of** ~の世話をする, ~の面倒を見る **take good care of** ~を大事に扱う, 大切にする **take off** （衣服を）脱ぐ, 取り去る, ~を取り除く **take one's eyes off** ~から目をそらす **take one's place** (人と) 交代する, (人の) 代わりをする, 後任になる **take out** 取り出す, 取り外す, 連れ出す, 持って帰る **take place** 行われる, 起こる **take someone away** (人)を連れ出す **take someone by the arm** (人) の腕を捕らえる, 腕をつかむ **take someone through** (人) に (場所) を通らせる **take ~ to ...** ~を…に連れて行く

☐ **taken by** 《be – 》~に魅せられる, 熱中する.

☐ **tale** 名①話, 物語 ②うわさ, 悪口

☐ **talk** 熟 **have a talk** 話をする

☐ **Tamba** 名丹波《地名》

☐ **tansu** 名箪笥

☐ **tatami** 名畳

☐ **tear apart** 引き裂く

☐ **tear off** 引きはがす

☐ **temple** 名寺

☐ **Tenno** 名天皇

☐ **terribly** 副ひどく

☐ **terror** 名①恐怖 ②恐ろしい人[物]

☐ **than** 熟 **more than** ~以上

☐ **thank ... for ~** ~に対して…に礼を言う

☐ **there** 熟 **get there** そこに到着する **there lived ~.** ~が住んでいました。

☐ **thereafter** 副それ以来, 従って

☐ **therefore** 副したがって, それゆえ, その結果

☐ **thin** 形薄い, 細い, やせた

☐ **think of** ~のことを考える, ~を思いつく, 考え出す

☐ **thinking** 名考えること, 思考

☐ **thirsty** 形①のどが渇いた ②渇望する

☐ **this** 熟 **like this** このような, こんなふうに

☐ **those** 熟 **in those days** あのころは, 当時は

☐ **though** 接①~にもかかわらず, ~だが ②たとえ~でも **come through** 通り抜ける **go through** 通り抜ける **look through** ~をのぞき込む **pass through** ~を通る, 通行する **take someone through** (人) に (場所) を通らせる

☐ **throw down** 投げ出す, 放棄する

☐ **thus** 副①このように ②これだけ ③かくて, だから

☐ **tightly** 副きつく, しっかり, 堅く

- **time** 熟 by the time 〜する時までに　some time later しばらくして
- **tiny** 形 ちっぽけな, とても小さい
- **tired** 形 ①疲れた, くたびれた ②あきた, うんざりした
- **Toichi** 名 十市《地名》
- **Tokoyo** 名 常世《古代伝説で海の彼方にあるとされていた国。または黄泉の国, 不老不死の国》
- **Tokyo** 名 東京《地名》
- **Tomotada** 名 友忠《人名》
- **too much** 過度の
- **too 〜 to ...** …するには〜すぎる
- **tool** 名 道具, 用具, 工具
- **training** 名 トレーニング, 訓練
- **traveling (Buddhist) priest** 旅僧
- **treat** 動 扱う
- **trial** 名 裁判
- **trouble** 熟 get into trouble 面倒を起こす, 困った事になる, トラブルに巻き込まれる
- **trust** 動 信用[信頼]する
- **truth** 名 真理, 事実, 本当
- **turn around** 振り向く, 向きを変える, 方向転換する
- **turn away** 向こうへ行く, 追い払う, (顔を)そむける, 横を向く
- **two** 熟 a 〜 or two 1〜か2〜, 2, 3の

U

- **uncombed** 形 (髪が)とかされていない, 乱れた
- **unhappy** 形 不運な, 不幸な
- **unless** 接 もし〜でなければ, 〜しなければ
- **unlock** 動 かぎを開ける, 解く
- **unlucky** 形 ①不運な ②不吉な, 縁起の悪い
- **unsui-no-ryokaku** 名 雲水の旅客《行方を定めず諸国を行脚する僧》
- **unworried** 形 心配していない
- **up** 熟 dig up 掘り起こす, 掘り出す　grow up 成長する, 大人になる　hurry up 急ぐ　jump up 素早く立ち上がる　look up 見上げる　pick up 拾い上げる, 車で迎えに行く, 習得する, 再開する, 回復する　run up 〜に走り寄る　stand up 立ち上がる　wake up 起きる, 目を覚ます
- **upon** 前 《場所・接触》〜 (の上) に
- **upper** 形 上の, 上位の, 北方の
- **upset** 形 憤慨して, 動揺して
- **upstairs** 副 2階へ[に], 階上へ
- **use** 熟 of no use 使われないで
- **used** 動 《 – to》よく〜したものだ, 以前は〜であった 形 慣れている, 《get [become] – to》〜に慣れてくる

V

- **vast** 形 広大な, 巨大な, ばく大な
- **vegetable** 名 野菜, 青物
- **very well** 結構, よろしい
- **visit** 熟 pay a visit 〜を訪問する
- **visitor** 名 訪問客

W

- **wait for** 〜を待つ
- **waiting** 形 待っている, 仕えている
- **wake up** 起きる, 目を覚ます
- **walk around** 歩き回る, ぶらぶら歩く
- **walk away** 立ち去る, 遠ざかる
- **walk on** 歩き続ける
- **walk over** 〜の方に歩いていく

□ **warn** 動警告する, 用心させる

□ **waterfall** 名滝

□ **wave** 名波

□ **way** 熟 along the way 途中で on one's way to ～に行く途中で on the way to ～へ行く途中で

□ **wealthy** 形裕福な, 金持ちの

□ **wedding** 名結婚式, 婚礼

□ **weep** 動しくしく泣く, 嘆き悲しむ

□ **well** 熟 as well なお, その上, 同様に very well 結構, よろしい

□ **well-dressed** 形きちんとした身なりの

□ **wet** 形ぬれた, 湿った

□ **whatever** 形①どんな～でも ②《否定文・疑問文で》少しの～も, 何らかの

□ **while** 熟 for a while しばらくの間, 少しの間

□ **whisper** 動ささやく, 小声で話す

□ **white** 熟 dress in white 白い服を着る

□ **whole** 形全体の, すべての

□ **wide** 形幅の広い, 広範囲の, 幅が～ある 副広く, 大きく開いて

□ **widowed** 形未亡人になった

□ **Will you ～?** 熟～してくれませんか。

□ **willow** 名ヤナギ(柳)

□ **wine** 名ワイン rice wine 日本酒

□ **wing** 名翼, 羽

□ **wipe** 動～をふく, ぬぐう, ふきとる

□ **wise** 形賢明な, 聡明な, 博学の

□ **wisely** 副賢明に

□ **without** 熟 go without ～なしですませる

□ **woke** 動 wake (目が覚める)の過去

□ **wonder** 動①不思議に思う, (～に)驚く ②(～かしらと)思う wonder if ～ではないかと思う

□ **woodcutter** 名きこり

□ **wooden** 形木製の, 木でできた

□ **worker** 名仕事をする人, 労働者

□ **worried** 形心配そうな, 不安げな

□ **worried about** 《be－》(～のことで)心配している, ～が気になる[かかる]

□ **worry about** ～のことを心配する

□ **worse** 形いっそう悪い, よりひどい

□ **would like** ～がほしい

□ **would like to** ～したいと思う

□ **wound** 名傷

□ **write to** ～に手紙を書く

□ **wrong with** 《be－》(～にとって)よくない

Y

□ **Yamato Province** 大和国《地名》

□ **yashiki** 名屋敷

□ **Yedo** 名江戸《地名》

□ **yet** 熟 not yet まだ～してない

□ **youth** 名若さ, 元気, 若者

□ **youthful** 形若々しい

□ **Yuki-Onna** 名雪女

Z

□ **Zen** 名禅

109

English Conversational Ability Test
国際英語会話能力検定

● E-CATとは…
英語が話せるようになるための
テストです。インターネット
ベースで、30分であなたの発
話力をチェックします。

www.ecatexam.com

● iTEP®とは…
世界各国の企業、政府機関、アメリカの大学
300校以上が、英語能力判定テストとして採用。
オンラインによる90分のテストで文法、リー
ディング、リスニング、ライティング、スピー
キングの5技能をスコア化。iTEP®は、留学、就
職、海外赴任などに必要な、世界に通用する英
語力を総合的に評価する画期的なテストです。

www.itepexamjapan.com

ラダーシリーズ

Kwaidan 怪談

2021年9月5日　第1刷発行

原著者　小泉八雲

発行者　浦　晋亮

発行所　IBCパブリッシング株式会社
　　　　〒162-0804 東京都新宿区中里町29番3号
　　　　菱秀神楽坂ビル9F
　　　　Tel. 03-3513-4511　Fax. 03-3513-4512
　　　　www.ibcpub.co.jp

印　刷　株式会社シナノパブリッシングプレス
装　丁　伊藤 理恵
イラスト　ミヤザーナツ

Printed in Japan
ISBN978-4-7946-0677-8